**THIRD EDITION**

# Writing Papers in Psychology

## A STUDENT GUIDE

Ralph L. Rosnow
*Temple University*

Mimi Rosnow

Brooks/Cole Publishing Company

I(T)P™ An International Thomson Publishing Company

Pacific Grove • Albany • Bonn • Boston • Cincinnati • Detroit • London • Madrid • Melbourne
Mexico City • New York • Paris • San Francisco • Singapore • Tokyo • Toronto • Washington

Sponsoring Editor: *Jim Brace-Thompson*
Marketing Representative: *Joyce Larcom*
Editorial Associate: *Cathleen S. Collins*
Production Editor: *Kirk Bomont*
Manuscript Editor: *Margaret Ritchie*
Permissions Editor: *Carline Haga*
Interior Design: *Vernon T. Boes*

Cover Design: *E. Kelly Shoemaker*
Cover Photo: *Telegraph Colour Library/FPG International*
Art Coordinator: *Susan H. Horovitz*
Typesetting: *Bookends Typesetting*
Printing and Binding: *Malloy Lithographing, Inc.*

*For more information, contact:*

BROOKS/COLE PUBLISHING COMPANY
511 Forest Lodge Road
Pacific Grove, CA 93950
USA

International Thomson Publishing Europe
Berkshire House 168–173
High Holborn
London WC1V 7AA
England

Thomas Nelson Australia
102 Dodds Street
South Melbourne, 3205
Victoria, Australia

Nelson Canada
1120 Birchmount Road
Scarborough, Ontario
Canada M1K 5G4

International Thomson Editores
Campos Eliseos 385, Piso 7
Col. Polanco
11560 México D. F. México

International Thomson Publishing GmbH
Königswinterer Strasse 418
53227 Bonn
Germany

International Thomson Publishing Asia
221 Henderson Road #05–10
Henderson Building
Singapore 0315

International Thomson Publishing Japan
Hirakawacho-cho Kyowa Building, 3F
2-2-1 Hirakawacho-cho
Chiyoda-ku, 102 Tokyo
Japan

Printed in the United States of America

10 9 8 7 6 5 4 3 2 1

**Library of Congress Cataloging-in-Publication Data**
Rosnow, Ralph L.
    Writing papers in psychology : a student guide / Ralph L. Rosnow, Mimi Rosnow. — 3rd ed.
        p.    cm.
    Includes index.
    ISBN 0-534-24378-9
    1. Psychology—Authorship.    2. Report writing.    I. Rosnow, Mimi, [date].    II. Title.
    BF76.7.R67    1995
    808'.06615—dc20

94-9163
CIP

To the partnership
that brought this book about

**Ralph L. Rosnow**

*teaches in the Psychology Department at Temple University
and has also taught at Boston University and Harvard
University. He has written numerous books and journal
articles on a wide variety of topics in psychology.*

**Mimi Rosnow**

*took her undergraduate degree in English at Wheaton College
in Norton, Massachusetts. She has done freelance editorial
consulting and for a number of years has been an editorial
assistant at a national magazine.*

# CONTENTS

CHAPTER ONE

## Getting Started      1

CHAPTER TWO

## Using the Library      12

CHAPTER THREE

# Outlining the Term Paper     **35**

CHAPTER FOUR

# Planning the Research Report     **42**

CHAPTER FIVE

# Writing and Revising     **51**

CHAPTER SIX

# Layout and Production                                        70

APPENDIX A

# Sample Term Paper                                            85

APPENDIX B

# Sample Research Report                                      101

# PREFACE

In the age of television pictures and the spoken word, most students feel a sense of apprehension when they know they have to express their thoughts in writing. Just as it requires less effort to pick up the telephone than to write a letter, it is often easier to talk about an idea than to compose and polish a written report. College students are not usually given this choice, however, but instead are required to develop and submit a number of formal reports. This manual speaks to students in psychology and related fields who are looking for a resource and guide to walk them through the steps in writing and submitting either a term paper or a report of empirical research. We hope the guidelines presented here will ease the process of communicating ideas effectively and will leave the student with a sense of satisfaction that comes with the mastery of effective written communication.

## Organization

Except for Chapters 3 and 4, the information presented is applicable to both the term paper and the research report. We contrast the two forms and explain how a student can proceed step-by-step from choosing a topic, using the library, structuring the paper, and writing and polishing it, to producing the final manuscript. We do not discuss the technical criteria of good scientific hypotheses (falsifiability, parsimony and cohesiveness, and so on) but assume that the student assigned to write a research report is being taught these basics with the aid of a research methods text. Although we mention a number of style tips, we also assume the student has been taught writing techniques. We did not want to burden students with a manual so technical and detailed that it could serve as a textbook in a course of instruction. For readers who want to brush up on basic writing skills, we recommend William Strunk Jr. and E. B. White's *The Elements of Style* (Macmillan).

Guided by the following flowchart, students can refer to specific chapters and sections as needed:

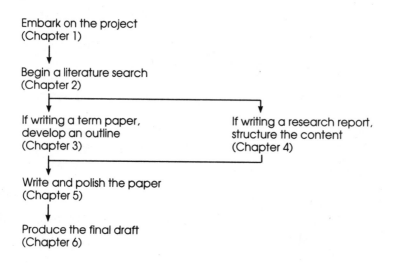

Embark on the project
(Chapter 1)

Begin a literature search
(Chapter 2)

If writing a term paper,
develop an outline
(Chapter 3)

If writing a research report,
structure the content
(Chapter 4)

Write and polish the paper
(Chapter 5)

Produce the final draft
(Chapter 6)

## New Features

Instructors familiar with the previous editions of this book will recognize a number of changes in this third edition. We have updated and expanded Chapter 2 on using the library by including new examples from *SSCI* and *Psychological Abstracts,* an example of ERIC for students who are writing on topics in education, and a discussion of the new technology that is available in many college libraries. Also new are pointers on how to locate hard-to-find work (called the *fugitive literature*) and a discussion of ethics in scientific writing, a timely topic in light of the 1993 revision by the American Psychological Association (APA) of its ethics code. Other sections that we have expanded include tips on nonsexist language, the use of a word processor, and writing style. At the same time, we have tried to simplify the layout of the final report based on feedback we have received from students and instructors. We invite users of this edition to send us their suggestions for future improvements.

## Recommended Style

We are sometimes asked why we did not simply replicate the APA style as spelled out in the *Publication Manual of the American*

*Psychological Association.* In fact, we have borrowed several of the reporting rules from that manual, but there are a number of reasons why we do not insist that student papers rigorously conform to APA guidelines. First, many students find it frustrating to comply with the style and formatting rules in the APA manual, and we did not want to sap their creative energy and enthusiasm by having them fixate on a very detailed set of publication rules. Second, while all the APA publication rules make a great deal of sense to psychological researchers, authors, and compositors, they have little meaning to most students (who are creating a manuscript for an instructor). Third, most instructors who teach research methods require that raw data, calculations, and questionnaires be submitted with the final report (typically in an appendix), whereas the APA manual proceeds on the assumption that research journals are pressed for space.

Of course, if students are interested in publication in a journal that uses the APA style, we always point them to the APA manual. Another useful text is Robert J. Sternberg's *The Psychologist's Companion,* published by Cambridge University Press. A particular favorite of ours, though it is not addressed specifically to psychologists, is Robert A. Day's *How to Publish a Scientific Paper,* published by the Institute for Scientific Information (ISI) in Philadelphia. If a student is using WordPerfect and having difficulty formatting the paper in APA style, we also recommend "Formatting APA Pages in WordPerfect 5.1," by Randolph A. Smith (*Teaching of Psychology,* 1992, vol. 19, pp. 190–191).

Among the basic differences that exist between the format prescribed here and that in the APA manual are the following: The cover page of student papers omits the short title over the page number (which some students find hard to set up on the word processor) and the running head. Instead, it should present information pertinent to the project and the course. On page 3, the title is not repeated, and instead a center heading appears (for example, "Introduction"); it is a constant reminder to the student of the purpose of this section. A table or figure is placed on the page following its discussion in the narrative and is usually referred to by a parenthetical note (for example, "see Table 1 on page 5"); underlining the title of the table is not recommended (the purpose of underlining is to instruct the compositor to put the title in italics). We do ask that letters used as statistical symbols or algebraic variables be underlined, simply because this underlining is an ingrained habit in our field and instructors have told us that research reports look "naked" without it. We also advise that the research report include an appendix containing statistical computations and any other relevant data or material required by the instructor. In most other respects, we have used APA style (for example, for references and citations).

## Choosing a Word Processor

We are often asked by students what word-processing system we recommend or what system we use. This manual was composed on a Jurassic-period IBM PC that we had reconfigured some years ago to bring it more up-to-date. We also used a still serviceable, but no longer popular, word-processing program (we won't mention the name) and at the end of each day printed a hard copy using an HP LaserJet. In other work, one of us uses another prehistoric IBM-compatible and a specialized program, while the other uses a somewhat more juiced IBM clone and a popular word-processing program that is useful for building statistical equations. When we are asked to recommend a system, we usually advise students to experiment with those at their college. We tell them to write down what they like or despise about each system and ask questions at computer stores, even if they don't intend to buy a system right away. These are good ways to begin to eliminate alternatives, as well as to become acquainted with the vernacular language of "computerese" (which can make a neophyte user's eyes spin). Having said this, we add that learning to use a word processor is an essential part of one's college education.

## Acknowledgments

We also have been asked whether "Maria" and "John"—who have achieved mythic proportions among some students—are real people or merely figments of our imagination. Maria DiMedio—now Dr. Maria Mastrippolito—took her Ph.D. in social psychology at Temple University in 1991. She then taught at Lincoln University and is now devoting much of her energy to raising two young children and developing the outline of a book. Her term paper in Appendix A was originally written when she was an undergraduate student at Cabrini College. She revised the current version of her paper to bring the literature review up-to-date. John H. Yost—now

Dr. Yost—did the original version of the research report in Appendix B while he was in the undergraduate honors program at Temple University. He then went on to Washington University in St. Louis, where in 1992 he took his Ph.D. in social psychology. He holds a postdoctoral fellowship in social psychology at Ohio State University. We thank these two real people for allowing us to edit their work and to include the edited versions as sample presentations in this manual.

We also thank MaryLu Rosenthal for advising us through all three editions about the methods and means available for a literature search in a modern college library. We thank Donna Shires (who is now completing her Ph.D. at Temple University in organizational-social psychology) for allowing us to incorporate her suggestions on how to use PsycLIT. We thank the many users of this manual, including a long line of graduate assistants and undergraduate students who provided valuable comments on the first and second editions. We thank the following consultants for constructive feedback during various phases in the development of one or more editions of this book: John B. Best, Eastern Illinois University; David Goldstein, Duke University; John Hall, Texas Wesleyan University; James W. Kalat, North Carolina State University; Allan J. Kimmel, Fitchburgh State College; Joann Montepare, Tufts University; Arthur Nonneman, Asbury College; Edgar O'Neal, Tulane University; Rick Pollack, Merrimack College; Maureen Powers, Vanderbilt University; Robert Rosenthal, Harvard University; Gordon W. Russell, University of Lethbridge; and John Sparrow, State University of New York at Geneseo. The first author also wishes to thank Ellen Irving in Temple University's Department of Psychology and information specialists at Paley Library for their helpful assistance. We thank Margaret Ritchie for her fine-tuning of our writing. We thank Ken King of Wadsworth for his support of the first two editions of this book, and we thank Jim Brace-Thompson of Brooks/Cole for his support of this latest edition.

We do not always specify publication dates for reference books in our own narrative; instead we advise students to seek the latest edition available and thus avoid consulting outdated material. In addition to the APA manual (which was useful in reminding us of technical points we might have forgotten to mention), we also found the following books helpful: R. Barrass, *Scientists Must Write* (Wiley, 1978); R. W. Bly and G. Blake, *Technical Writing: Structure, Standard, and Style* (McGraw-Hill, 1982); V. Dumond, *Elements of Nonsexist*

*Usage: A Guide to Inclusive Spoken and Written English* (Prentice-Hall, 1990); B. L. Ellis, *How to Write Themes and Term Papers* (Barron's, 1989); D. E. Fear, *Technical Writing* (Random House, 1973); H. R. Fowler, *The Little, Brown Handbook* (Little, Brown, 1983); J. Gibaldi and W. S. Achtert, *MLA Handbook for Writers of Research Papers* (Modern Language Association, 1988); K. W. Houp and T. E. Pearsall, *Reporting Technical Information* (Macmillan, 1984); C. Hult and J. Harris, *A Writer's Introduction to Word Processing* (Wadsworth, 1987); S. Kaye, *Writing Under Pressure: The Quick Writing Process* (Oxford University Press, 1989); M. H. Markel, *Technical Writing: Situations and Strategies* (St. Martin's, 1984); M. McCormick, *The New York Times Guide to Reference Materials* (Dorset, 1985); D. J. D. Mulkerne and D. J. D. Mulkerne Jr., *The Term Paper* (Anchor/Doubleday, 1983); L. A. Olsen and T. N. Huchin, *Principles of Communication for Science and Technology* (McGraw-Hill, 1957); J. G. Reed and P. M. Baxter, *Library Use: A Handbook for Psychology* (American Psychological Association, 1992); B. Spatt, *Writing from Sources* (St. Martin's, 1987); K. L. Turabian, *A Manual for Writers of Term Papers, Theses and Dissertations* (University of Chicago Press, 1955); and J. E. Warriner, *Handbook of English* (Harcourt, Brace, 1951).

*Ralph L. Rosnow*
*Mimi Rosnow*

---

# CHAPTER ONE

# Getting Started

*The term paper and the research report are distinctly different forms that share certain similarities. Both have a relatively simple format; both are written for a specific reader, the instructor; and both require that the steps in the project be paced so that the assignment, completed on time, represents your best work. This chapter focuses on the rudiments of getting started: that is, helping you know where you are heading and formulating a plan to get you there on schedule.*

## Knowing Your Objective

Before you turn on a word processor or begin to sharpen any pencils, ask yourself this question:

Do I understand the assignment?

If you are not *sure* of the answer, ask the instructor what is expected of you. You can talk with other students to get their impressions, but the instructor is the only person who can describe the assignment accurately. Most instructors find that one student in every class goes off on a tangent and then suffers the consequences of a low grade. Don't let that student be you!

Here is a checklist of questions that you might ask yourself before proceeding:

- ➤ What is the objective of the writing assignment?
- ➤ Do I choose the theme or topic, or will it be assigned by the instructor?
- ➤ How long should the paper be?
- ➤ Will progress reports be required? If so, when?
- ➤ When is the final report due?

A sense of the difference between the term paper and the research report (see Exhibit 1) will help you focus your efforts on whichever project you have been assigned.

One distinction highlighted in the Exhibit 1 table is that a literature search usually forms the core of the term paper, while data form the core of the research report. The literature search for the research report typically involves only a few key studies that serve as a theoretical starting point, so you can expect to spend a lot more time in the library if you are writing a term paper. Of course, you still must spend time in the library if you are writing a research report, because you will need to look up background information.

A second distinction is that the composition of the term paper, although somewhat formal, is more flexible than that of the research report, which has a much more standardized structure. Term papers are relatively flexible because there are different types that represent widely different objectives. Most instructors expect the structure of the research report to conform to a general tradition that has evolved over many years. As a consequence, research reports typically include an abstract (that is, a brief summary), an introduction,

**EXHIBIT 1** Differences between term papers and research reports

| Term Paper | Research Report |
|---|---|
| 1. Based on literature search; no hard data of your own to interpret | 1. Based on data that you have collected; literature search involving only a few key studies |
| 2. Structured by you to fit your particular topic | 2. Structured following a traditional form |
| 3. Puts ideas into the context of a particular thesis | 3. Reports your own research findings to others |

a method section, a results section, a discussion of the results, and a list of the references cited.

The final distinction noted in Exhibit 1 is that the term paper puts issues and ideas into the context of a particular theme or thesis, whereas the objective of the research report is to describe your empirical investigation to others. We will have more to say about this last point later.

## Three Types of Term Papers

There are three basic types of term papers—expository, argumentative, and descriptive—and each has its own objective.

First, the **expository term paper** is illustrated by Maria Di Medio's essay in Appendix A (beginning on page 86). The word *expository* means "to expound," "set forth," or "explain," and the purpose of this kind of paper is to inform the reader on a specific subject or theme—in Maria's case, two therapeutic approaches to treating anorexia nervosa. Such papers call for simplicity in writing—like the articles that are in the science section of the *New York Times* each Tuesday, but in more detail and with full citations. Maria does not begin by writing, "I am going to explain how anorexia nervosa is treated." That is, in fact, her aim (implicit in the title of her paper), but her opening sentence is more polished and interesting. Other examples of expository term papers might be "Theories of Rumor Generation and Transmission"; "Basic Differences Between Operant and Classical Conditioning"; "Role of the Teacher's Expectations in Students' Academic Performance." Each paper promises to inform the reader about some topic but will not necessarily assert or challenge a particular point of view.

Second, the object of persuading the reader to accept a particular point of view calls for an **argumentative term paper.** For example, you might write an essay asserting the cost-effectiveness of behavior therapy as opposed to some other psychotherapeutic approach, or you might write a paper that challenges the applicability of some theory in a realm beyond that for which it was originally intended. This type of paper asks the reader to form a new view or change his or her mind on a particular issue. As in any fair argument, all viewpoints should be represented, and not just in a "take it or leave it" fashion. Show that you recognize gray areas as you develop your position, and present significant documentation to support it. If you are arguing against a particular viewpoint, collect specific quotations of that view to illustrate that you have represented it accurately. Otherwise, you may be accused of making a "straw man" argument, which means that you have represented the other side in a false, unfair, or misleading way to buttress your personal view. It can be helpful to argue one's point of view with someone who is a good listener and promises to be very critical; jot down that person's questions and counterarguments while they are fresh in your mind so that you can deal with them in your paper.

Third, the purpose of the **descriptive term paper** is to map out its subject, to express how things are. Examples include a case study involving some personal experience or a narrative interpretation of a particular event. If you were writing a descriptive essay in an English course, you would have an opportunity to exercise your creative ability. Creativity is also valued in science, but when describing things, you want to be accurate and not take a flight of fancy. An effective descriptive essay in psychology is not vague; it incorporates specific examples and faithful quotations to support ideas. You will find fascinating examples of such essays in the annals of clinical psychology and psychiatry, such as Sigmund Freud's famous study of the "Wolf-Man," a Russian aristocrat who as a youth developed a wolf phobia and as an adult was psychoanalyzed by Freud.

Incidentally, whichever type of paper you have been assigned to write, most term papers are 15 to 20 pages long (not counting the reference section). Maria's paper in Appendix A illustrates the recommended format of an expository paper, but not necessarily its recommended length.

## Three Types of Research Reports

Researchers make fine distinctions among the various kinds of research approaches (for example, the laboratory experiment, the field experiment, the sample survey approach, the intensive case study), but it is convenient to boil them down to three general types: descriptive, relational, and experimental. The structure of the research report is similar in each case, but the objective of the report is different.

First, the purpose of the **descriptive research report** (like that of the descriptive term paper) is to map out its subject. For example, you might report the observations you made of freshman students thrown together for the first time as roommates in a dormitory or perhaps of people who have been hypnotized for the first time. Another illustration of descriptive research would be an educational psychologist who is interested in studying children's failure in school. The researcher might begin by spending a good deal of time observing the classroom behavior of children who are doing poorly. The researcher then would carefully describe what was observed. Careful description of failing pupils might lead to ideas about how to revise our concepts of classroom failure, to suggestions of factors that may have contributed to the development of failure, and perhaps to innovative hypotheses concerning the remediation of failure.

The careful description of behavior is a necessary first step in the development of a program of research. Sooner or later, however, someone will want to know *how* what happens behaviorally is related to other variables. That is the objective of the **relational research report,** which examines how events are related or how behavior is correlated with another variable. For instance, you might report on how first-year college students behaved differently toward one another over time or how subjects of hypnosis gradually learned to respond in a certain way; the factor of time or the number of sessions would be one variable, and behavior would be the correlated variable. In Appendix B, John Yost's report (beginning on page 102) is an example of relational (also called *correlational*) research. John examines differences in people's self-reported confidence in rumors and how such differences are correlated with rumor transmission. The researcher interested in failure in school might note for each pupil (1) whether the child was learning anything or the degree to which the child had been learning and (2) the degree to which the teacher had been exposing the child to the material to be learned. The finished report would examine the relationship between the amount of the pupils' exposure to the material to be learned and the amount of such material that they did in fact learn.

Third is the **experimental research report.** We implied that descriptive reports examine *how things are* and that relational reports examine *how things are in relation to other things.* The purpose of the experimental report is to examine *how things get to be the way they are.* For example, you might report on how social behavior in rats is affected when the experimenter manipulates the animals' reinforcement schedules. If John's study whets your interest in the psychology of rumor, you might design an experiment to try to reveal the causal association implied between the degree of confidence in a rumor and the likelihood of its transmission. In the case of children's failure, the researcher might examine whether teachers actually teach less to pupils whom they believe to be less able to learn. In the finished report, the researcher would concentrate on the question "What leads to what?" in the situation of pupil failure as a function of teachers' expectations of failure.

## Scheduling Time

The next step is to set some deadlines. In *The Shaping of a Behaviorist* (New York University Press, 1984), the eminent psychologist B. F. Skinner recollected how he had sought to discipline himself by developing a very strict regimen when he entered Harvard University as a graduate student in 1928:

> I had done what was expected of me in high school and college but had seldom worked hard. Aware that I was far behind in a new field, I now set up a rigorous schedule and maintained it for almost two years. I would rise at six, study until breakfast, go to classes, laboratories, and libraries with no more than fifteen minutes unscheduled during the day, study until exactly nine o'clock at night and go to bed. (p. 5)

No one expects you to develop a schedule as stringent as Professor Skinner's when he was a student. However, once you feel that you know what is expected of you, it is time to set specific deadlines that you feel you can meet. You know your own energy level and thought patterns, so play to your strengths. Are you a morning person? If so, block out some time to work on your paper early in the day. Do you function better at night? Then use the late hours of quiet to your advantage. Allow extra time for other pursuits by setting realistic dates by which you can reasonably expect to complete each major part of your assignment. Write the dates on your calendar; many students also find it useful to post the dates over their desks as daily reminders.

How do you know what tasks to schedule? If you look again at Maria's and John's papers in Appendixes A and B, you will see that writing a term paper calls for a different schedule from writing a research report. As we said, writing a term paper requires spending a lot of time in the library accumulating source materials, so you will need to leave ample time for that task. Here are some hints about what to schedule in your calendar:

> Completion of outline of term paper
> Completion of library work
> Completion of first draft of term paper
> Completion of revised draft(s) of term paper
> Completion of final draft of term paper

If you are assigned a research report, set aside ample time for these major tasks:

> Completion of proposal for research
> Completion of data collection
> Completion of data analysis
> Completion of first draft of research report
> Completion of revised draft(s) of research report
> Completion of final draft of research report

By scheduling your time in this way, you will not feel pressured by imaginary deadlines or surprised as the real deadline approaches. Get started right away—don't procrastinate. Organizing, writing, and revising will take time. Library research does not always go smoothly; a book or journal article you need might be unavailable. Data collection and analysis also can run into snags: research subjects might not cooperate, or a computer you need might be down.

If you get started early, you also will have time to track down hard-to-find reports (called the *fugitive literature* in Chapter 2) or to write to authors for follow-up articles if you think you need them. (Many students are surprised to learn that they can actually write to an author of a research study and ask about the author's most recent work.) If you want to use a published test or questionnaire in your research, you need to give yourself time to locate a copy and (maybe) get permission to use the instrument.

Note that both schedules of tasks allow time between the first and final drafts to distance yourself from your writing. This time allows you to return to your project with a fresh perspective as you polish the first draft and check for errors in logic, flow, spelling, punctuation, and grammar. Another word of advice: instructors have heard all the excuses for a late or badly done paper, so do not expect much sympathy if you miss the final deadline. If you expect to ask the instructor for a letter of recommendation to graduate school or a job, you certainly do not want to leave her or him with an impression of you as unreliable, or as unable to meet deadlines.

## Choosing a Topic

The next step is to choose a suitable topic. The selection of a topic is an integral part of learning, because usually you are free to explore experiences, observations, and ideas to help you focus on specific questions or issues that will sustain your curiosity and interest as you work on your project. In considering a suitable topic, beware of a few pitfalls; the following are "dos" and "don'ts" that might make your life easier as you start choosing a topic:

➤ Be enthusiastic and strive for a positive attitude.
➤ Use the indexes and tables of contents of standard textbooks as well as class notes for initial leads or ideas you would like to explore more fully.
➤ Choose a topic that piques your curiosity.
➤ Make sure your topic can be covered in the available time and the assigned number of pages.
➤ Don't be afraid to ask your instructor for suggestions.
➤ Don't choose a topic that you know other students have chosen; you will be competing with them for access to the library's source material—as well as for a good grade.

## Shaping the Topic

Choosing too broad or too narrow a topic for a term paper or research report will surely add difficulties and will also mean an unsatisfactory result. A term paper that is too broad—for example, "Freud's Life and Times"—would try to cover too much material within the limited framework of the assignment and the time available to complete it. A specific aspect of Freud's life and times would prove a more appropriately narrowed focus for treatment in a term paper.

However, in narrowing the topic, do not limit your discussion just to facts that are already well known. There are two simple guidelines:

➤ Be sure that your topic is not so narrow that reference materials will be hard to find.

➤ Be guided by your instructor's advice.

If you approach instructors with several concrete ideas, you will usually find them glad to help tailor those ideas so that you, the topic, and the project format are compatible.

Here are examples of how you might shape the topic about Sigmund Freud by a specific working title:

## Unlimited Topic (Much Too Broad)

"Life and Times of Sigmund Freud"

## Slightly Limited Topic (Still Too Broad)

"Psychological Theories of Sigmund Freud"

## Limited to 20-Page Paper

"Freud's Theory of Personality Applied to Mental Health"

## Limited to 10-Page Paper

"Freud's Theory of Infantile Sexuality"

## Too Narrow a Topic

"Freud's Pets"

You can always polish the title later, once you have finished your library search and have a better sense of the topic.

Here is another example of shaping a topic. This time the assignment is a research project, and the student must choose a topic in an area of social psychology:

## Unlimited Topic (Too Broad for a Term Project)

"Who Gossips and Why?"

## Slightly Limited Topic (Still Too Broad)

"When Do People Gossip?"

## Adequately Limited Topic

"Content Analysis of Selected Gossip Columns over a Specified Period"

# Knowing Your Audience and Topic

All professional writers know that they are writing for a particular audience. This knowledge helps them determine the tone and style of their work. Think of a journalist's report of a house fire and contrast it with a short story describing the same event. Knowing your audience is no less important when the writer is a college student and the project is a term paper or a research report. The audience is your instructor. Should you have any questions about the instructor's standards and expectations, find out what they are before you start to work.

For example, in a course on research methods taught by one instructor, the students were told that the grading criteria for different parts of the finished report would be as follows:

**Abstract**
    informativeness (5 points)
**Introduction**
    clarity of purpose (10)
    literature review (10)
**Method**
    adequacy of design (10)
    quality and completeness of description (10)
**Results**
    appropriateness and correctness of analysis (10)
    use of tables or figures (5)
    clarity of presentation (10)
**Discussion**
    interpretation of results (10)
    critique/future directions (10)
**Miscellaneous**
    organization, style, and so on (5)
    appendix (5)

This kind of information enabled the students to concentrate on different parts of the assignment in the same way that the instructor would concentrate on them when evaluating the reports.

This information can also serve as a checklist for you to make sure that everything of importance is covered adequately in your finished report. Not every instructor will provide such detailed information about grading, but this manual can help you compose your own refined checklist.

# Cultivating a Sense of Understanding

Let us assume that you know your audience: your instructor. Now you must try to develop more than just a superficial understanding of your topic. The more you read about it and discuss your ideas with friends, the more you will begin to cultivate an intuitive understanding of the topic. In the next chapter we describe how to use library resources to nurture this understanding. To help you get started, here are three tips:

➤ Many writers find it helpful to keep several 3 × 5-inch cards handy for jotting down relevant ideas that suddenly occur to them. This is a good way to keep your subject squarely in your mind.

➤ You must also comprehend your source material, so equip yourself with a good desk dictionary, and turn to it routinely whenever you come across an unfamiliar word. It is a habit that will serve you well.

➤ While you shop for a dictionary, you might also buy a thesaurus. It can be useful as an index of terms in information retrieval (discussed in Chapter 2) as well as a treasury of synonyms and antonyms when you write.

# CHAPTER TWO

# Using the Library

*Knowing about the many resources available in the library and knowing how to use them will prove invaluable to you. Familiarity with the many recent technological advances in library research will save time and effort. This chapter considers traditional and innovative resources to help you use the library most effectively.*

## Plan of the Library

If you have not set foot in your college library, begin by familiarizing yourself with the floor plan to find out where its major sections are. You can ask at the information desk whether there is a fact sheet that describes where to find things. You can also make up your own floor plan as you begin to orient yourself. It is not convenient to return to the information desk every time you have a question, so be aware of other places you can turn to for assistance.

Staff members (often called *information specialists*) also are available in specialized areas of the library. For example, many libraries have a **reference desk** and a **catalog desk,** although in some libraries the latter has been replaced by desktop computers. Whatever the name of the area, each provides specialized help in orienting patrons to the resources at hand. Don't be afraid to ask for guidance; librarians derive personal and professional satisfaction from being helpful and informative.

Here are some questions and tips to get you started:

➤ Where is the **information desk**? This is a general assistance area; the name speaks for itself. The staff members at this desk will refer you to the appropriate section of the library to find particular source material or to the appropriate librarian who can answer your specific questions. While you are here, find out what days and hours the library is open.

➤ Where is the **reference desk**? Staff members at this desk are true generalists who can either answer all manner of questions or point you to sources that will help you answer them yourself. They may, for example, suggest general reference works such as *Psychological Abstracts*, ERIC, or the *Social Sciences Citation Index*. Because this material is "not circulated" (not available to be checked out), you will have to work within a specified section of the library.

➤ Where is the **catalog desk**? This is the heart of the library; the card catalog is usually located nearby. The staff members at this desk can assist you in using the **card catalog** or the **online catalog** (the card catalog accessed by a computer), but many of your questions will also be answered in this chapter.

➤ Where is the **circulation desk**? This is where you check out books and other material. Bring an ID with you.

➤ Where is the **reserve area**? This is for books, photocopies of journal articles, tests, and so on that your instructor has placed "on hold" (not circulated). You can examine this material only in the library.

➤ How are the stacks of books arranged by call letters, and are you allowed to browse? Is a sequence of call numbers located on one floor or in one area and another sequence of call letters located elsewhere?

➤ Where is the **current periodicals area**? This is where you will find recent issues of journals, magazines, and newspapers. In libraries of the future (called *virtual libraries*), it is possible that journals and periodicals (and maybe even books) will be perused electronically, a process that will conserve space and avoid the problem of missing or damaged copies.

➤ Where are the **photocopiers** located? Do you need to bring coins or purchase a card in order to use them?

➤ Where do you find out about **interlibrary loan**? This is where you ask about borrowing material that is not available in your library. Is there a sample request form you can have?

➤ Is there a special area for **micromaterials**? Some documents are stored on microfilm and microfiche. Ask how to print out such material.

## How Material Is Cataloged

There are two easy-to-use sources of information on what is available in the library: the card catalog and the online catalog (if such a system is available). The *card catalog* is another name for the miles and miles of index cards that appear in alphabetical order in file drawers. The online catalog is a user-friendly, menu-driven computerized system that provides access to the same information by having you key in the answers to simple questions shown on the screen. In some libraries, the card catalog has actually disappeared and patrons have to use the online catalog to access information.

Some online catalogs are designed specifically for a given library, and some are generic designs sold by vendors. Some of these systems leave a lot to be desired, but most college and community libraries are trying to replace the card catalog with computerized systems, particularly for their current acquisitions. Online catalogs make life easier for library staff members (who must maintain the catalog) and also make life easier for patrons. You will probably not have to enter a complete title, author, or subject, but only type in a word, a last name, or a phrase. The computer will then help you find what you are looking for; typically there is a "Help" key you can press if you get confused. The simplest way to find out just how easy it is to use a computerized system is to try it.

As noted, the card catalog (on which the computerized system is based) is a file of alphabetized 3 × 5-inch cards. The cards tell you what is in the library and where to find it. Some libraries list periodicals (journals, magazines, and newspapers) separately in a serials catalog (possibly in a book or microfilm format of alphabetized listings).

Suppose you wanted to check out *Pygmalion in the Classroom,* a classic book by Robert Rosenthal and Lenore Jacobson. The library's books are usually entered on three types of catalog cards: (1) author cards, (2) title cards, and (3) subject cards. If you looked in the card file under either "Rosenthal, Robert" or "Jacobson, Lenore" (author card) or *"Pygmalion in the Classroom"* (title card), you would find a **call number** indicating where this book is stored in the library stacks (the shelves throughout the library). The stacks are coded according to categories that coincide with the numbers and letters on the index card in the card catalog or on the computer screen. To help locate the right book, the call number also appears at the bottom of the book's spine.

The author card for Rosenthal and Jacobson's *Pygmalion in the Classroom* is shown in Exhibit 2. The information in the upper-left corner is the call number: a sequence of letters and numbers specified by the Library of Congress to identify this work.

With few exceptions, each item held by the library (textbooks, reference works, phonograph records, disks and tapes, VCR and motion-picture films, and so on) has a catalog card that gives a full description of the material and its call number. To find out whether your library has the book you are looking for, you need only the name of one author or the title of the work. Without such information you can let your fingers do the walking through the appropriate

**EXHIBIT 2** Sample catalog card

| | |
|---|---|
| LB | **Rosenthal, Robert,** 1933— |
| 1131 | Pygmalion in the classroom; teacher expectation and pupils' |
| R585 | intellectual development [by] Robert Rosenthal [and] Lenore |
| | Jacobson. New York, Holt, Rinehart and Winston [1968] |
| | xi, 240 p. illus. 23 cm |
| | Bibliography: p. 219–229. |

1. Prediction of scholastic success. 2. Mental tests. I. Jacobson, Lenore, joint author. II. Title.

LB1131.R585        372.1'2'644        68–19667

Library of Congress

**EXHIBIT 3** Two systems of classification

| Library of Congress System | Dewey Decimal System |
|---|---|
| A General works | 000 General works |
| B Philosophy and religion | 100 Philosophy |
| C General history | 200 Religion |
| D Foreign history | 300 Social sciences |
| E-F America | 400 Language |
| G Geography and anthropology | 500 Natural sciences |
| H Social sciences | 600 Technology |
| J Political science | 700 Fine arts |
| K Law | 800 Literature |
| L Education | 900 History and geography |
| M Music | |
| N Fine arts | |
| P Language and literature | |
| Q Science | |
| R Medicine | |
| S Agriculture | |
| T Technology | |
| U Military science | |
| V Naval science | |
| Z Bibliography and library science | |

subject cards until you have located the work in question. As noted previously, you can also ask the computer (that is, the online catalog) to do the walking for you by telling it to find all the records beginning with the word, name, or phrase you have typed.

Exhibit 3 shows the two systems of classification most frequently used in U.S. libraries. For psychology students these can be puzzling systems because psychological material is classified under several different headings. The Library of Congress system divides material into 20 major groups, and abnormal psychology books, for example, can be found under BF or RC. The Dewey Decimal System classifies material under 10 headings (and abnormal psychology can be found in the 157 class).

If you are allowed to browse in the stacks, refer to Exhibit 4. It shows the cataloging of more specific areas by both systems. Browsing can lead you to a valuable but unexpected book or to a pungent quote to illustrate some idea or point.

If we go back to Exhibit 2, the call number of Rosenthal and Jacobson's book tells us that we would first go to the LB section of the stacks and next to the more specific section in numerical (1131)

**EXHIBIT 4**   Cataloging of psychological materials

| Library of Congress System | Dewey Decimal System |
|---|---|
| BF  Abnormal psychology | 00- Artificial intelligence |
|      Child psychology | 13- Parapsychology |
|      Cognition | 15- Abnormal psychology |
|      Comparative psychology |      Child psychology |
|      Environmental psychology |      Cognitive psychology |
|      Motivation |      Comparative psychology |
|      Parapsychology |      Environmental psychology |
|      Perception |      Industrial psychology |
|      Personality |      Motivation |
|      Physiological psychology |      Perception |
|      Psycholinguistics |      Personality |
|      Psychological statistics |      Physiological psychology |
| HF  Industrial psychology | 30- Family |
|      Personnel management |      Psychology of women |
| HM  Social psychology |      Social psychology |
| HQ  Family | 37- Educational psychology |
|      Psychology of women |      Special education |
| LB  Educational psychology | 40- Psycholinguistics |
| LC  Special education | 51- Statistics |
| Q  Artificial intelligence | 61- Psychiatry |
|      Physiological psychology |      Psychotherapy |
| QA  Mathematical statistics | 65- Personnel management |
| RC  Abnormal psychology | |
|      Psychiatry | |
|      Psychotherapy | |
| T  Personnel management | |

and then alphanumerical order (R585) where this book is shelved. The card also shows the name and birth year of the first author (Rosenthal, Robert, 1933–). Beneath are the title of the work and its subtitle ("teacher expectation and pupils' intellectual development"), followed by the complete list of authors in the order in which they appear on the title page of the work. Then follows the location and name of the publisher (New York, Holt, Rinehart and Winston) and the date of copyright (1968).

The remainder of the card lists further technical facts for librarians. The information in the middle of the card shows the number of prefatory pages (xi) and the length of the book (240 p.); it also indicates that the book contains figures or other illustrations (illus.), that it stands 23 cm. high on the shelf, and that the bibliography or list of references is on pages 219–229. The section below indicates the categories under which this book should be cataloged ("Mental tests," for example). Next is the book's Library of Congress classification number again (LB1131.R585), the Dewey Decimal System classification number of this work (372.1'2'644), the order number of this particular set of cards (68-19667), and from whom the cards can be ordered (Library of Congress).

# Doing a Literature Search

Let us explore some ways you might look for literature related to your project. You can do a hand search (which means you might take notes from a digest or a compendium of abstracts), or you can use a machine-readable database (which means using a computer terminal to access this information). The latter is easier and quicker because it allows the user to combine certain subject terms and to exclude unwanted terms.

Database systems use two basic approaches: the online and the compact disc. Besides being found in the printed format of *Psychological Abstracts* (which we describe later), the abstract is available in both computer formats. The online system is called PsycINFO, and the compact disc system is called PsycLIT. As a librarian friend put it, the advantage of the compact disc system is that patrons can search to their hearts' content, and librarians do not see all those dollar signs flying around in their heads. As the name implies, the compact disc format of *Psychological Abstracts* (PsycLIT) uses a removable disc to store information. Updated discs are purchased by the library from the American Psychological Association (APA). Incidentally, if you have a home computer with a modem, you can arrange to access PsycINFO through an 800 number that you can obtain from the American Psychological Association (when you call, ask how to sign up for a password to use the PsycINFO Actionline).

We will have more to say about PsycLIT later, but suppose all you need are four or five key citations to provide the basis for a working hypothesis in the introductory section of your research report. If you intend to do a hand search, a good place to look for key studies is the reference section or bibliography section of a current textbook or serial such as the *Annual Review of Psychology*. Another source of references on specific topics is the *Psychological Bulletin*, a journal of literature reviews; the last issue of every volume has an index. However, do not simply make a citation list of articles because your instructor will wonder if you have even read the studies cited. *Read the original work.*

Most students do not find the literature search an onerous task, but some have the feeling that they are being asked to climb Mount Everest without a Sherpa guide. If this describes you, then ask your instructor for some leads before you exhaust yourself searching aimlessly in the library for just the right reference or bibliography section. For example, the card in Exhibit 2 notes that this book contains an 11-page bibliography. But this book is so old (see the copyright date on the catalog card) that the list of references will not be of much help. In fact, a much easier way to get current information would be to use the *Social Sciences Citation Index* and PsycLIT.

Suppose you were looking for a general reference work, an encyclopedia of psychology. There are, in fact, many older and newer encyclopedias, including Benjamin B. Wolman's *International Encyclopedia of Psychiatry, Psychology, Psychoanalysis, and Neurology* (Van Nostrand Reinhold), Raymond J. Corsini's *Encyclopedia of Psychology* (Wiley), and H. J. Eysenck, W. Arnold, and R. Meili's *Encyclopedia of Psychology* (Herder and Herder). Other multivolume reference works that are relevant to psychology include *The Encyclopedia of Education* (Macmillan and Free Press) and the *International Encyclopedia of Communications* (Oxford University Press). Once you find where these volumes are stored, you can browse around for other, possibly more recent, references shelved nearby. Incidentally, if you happen to be looking for a reference book *about* the reference books available in your field, ask an information librarian for E. P. Sheehy's *Guide to Reference Books.* This is a comprehensive, annotated listing of reference books; if you simply ask for "Sheehy's," the librarian will know what you mean.

Our librarian friend reminds us to emphasize that librarians are highly skilled in helping students find material. No matter how much paperwork the librarian has on the desk and no matter how busy the librarian looks, students should not be intimidated. Do not be afraid to approach a librarian for help, because that is the librarian's main purpose.

## Indexes and Abstracts

Suppose you found a useful article or book that was published in 1968; its reference list sent you to related publications from 1968

**EXHIBIT 5** *SSCI* citations of *Pygmalion in the Classroom* in 1992*

| 68 Pygmalion Classroom | | | | | |
|---|---|---|---|---|---|
| Ambady N | Psychol B | 111 | 256 | 92 | R |
| Aronson JM | J Exp S Psy | 28 | 277 | 92 | |
| Berliner DC | Educ Psych | 27 | 143 | 92 | |
| Carnelle KB | J Soc Pers | 9 | 5 | 92 | |
| Deci EL | Educ Psych | 26 | 325 | 91 | |
| Ensminge ME | Sociol Educ | 65 | 95 | 92 | |
| Epstein EH | Ox Rev Educ | 18 | 201 | 92 | |
| Feingold A | Psychol B | 111 | 304 | 92 | R |
| Gaynor JLR | J Creat Beh | 26 | 108 | 92 | |
| Goldenbe C | Am Educ Res | 29 | 517 | 92 | |
| Haring KA | T Ear Child | 12 | 151 | 92 | |
| Jussim L | J Pers Soc | 62 | 402 | 92 | |
| " | " | 63 | 947 | 92 | |
| Kershaw T | J Black St | 23 | 152 | 92 | |
| Kravetz S | Res Dev Dis | 13 | 145 | 92 | |
| Mayes LC | J Am Med A | 267 | 406 | 92 | |
| McDiarmi GW | J Teach Edu | 43 | 83 | 92 | |
| McGorry PD | Aust Nz J P | 26 | 3 | 92 | R |
| Milich R | Sch Psych R | 21 | 400 | 92 | |
| Musser LM | Bas Appl PS | 12 | 441 | 91 | |
| Schwartz CA | Library Q | 62 | 123 | 92 | R |
| Semmel MI | J Spec Educ | 25 | 415 | 92 | |
| Spangenb ER | J Publ Pol | 11 | 26 | 92 | |
| Suen HK | T Ear Child | 12 | 66 | 92 | |

and earlier. To find more recent publications on the topic, you could turn to the *Social Sciences Citation Index (SSCI)*. This continuously updated series of volumes consists of three separate but related indexes to the behavioral and social science literature as far back as 1966. It shows—in alphabetical order, by the last name of the principal author (the first author)—the year's published literature that cited the work.

For example, if you looked up Rosenthal and Jacobson's *Pygmalion in the Classroom* in the *Social Sciences Citation Index 1992 Annual*, under Robert Rosenthal's name you would find the list of entries shown in Exhibit 5. Each entry gives the author of a work that refers to this book (for example, Ambady, N.), the source of the work (*Psychological Bulletin*), the volume number (111), the beginning page number (256), the year of publication (1992), and, in this case, a code letter (*R*) designating that the work was a review of the literature. Other code letters used by the SSCI are *C* for corrections; *D* for discussions (conference items); *L* for letters; *M* for meeting abstracts; *N* for technical notes; *RP* for reprint; and *W* for computer reviews (hardware, software, and database reviews).

The lack of a code letter tells us that the work is an article, report, technical paper, or the like. The fact that Ambady's work is current and a review article will make the task of doing a literature search much easier. You can now go to the periodicals section of the library and read both Ambady's article and any relevant references cited. Incidentally, a companion index, the *Science Citation Index* (*SCI*), also lists citations of works not usually indexed in the *SSCI*, so it may pay you to look in both the *SCI* and the *SSCI*.

## *Psychological Abstracts,* ERIC, and Other Indexes

*Psychological Abstracts,* on which PsycLIT is based, gives synopses of thousands of works in psychology and related disciplines. Exhibit 6 shows a sample of the wide range of works available in this resource, including four abstracts from a volume of *Psychological Abstracts* published in 1993: (1) an article by Anastasi (in a European journal) on the history of differential psychology; (2) a book by Spiegelman on Judaism and Jungian psychology; (3) a chapter by Foster and Brizius on women's issues; and (4) a journal article by Draper on working conditions and industrial safety. Each example contains information about the particular work.

For instance, Anastasi's abstract begins with a code number (27890), so you can easily find the abstract again by going back to this volume and looking up this code number. The author's name is then listed; if there were more than four authors, the fourth would be followed by "et al." The first author's affiliation is given next, and then the work's title is shown, followed by the journal (or other) source in which the work appeared. If the work was based on some previously published entry in *Psychological Abstracts,* that information appears next. A synopsis of the work follows; next are the number of references and the source of the abstract. The "German abstract" in parentheses tells us that the abstract appears in a different language from that of the original work.

The abstract of Spiegelman's book also contains the table of contents and a note indicating that the synopsis is from publicity

**EXHIBIT 6**   Sample abstracts from *Psychological Abstracts**

27890. **Anastasi, Anne.** (Fordham U, NY) **The differential orientation in psychology.** *Zeitschrift für Differentielle und Diagnostische Psychologie,* 1992 (Sep), Vol 13(3), 133–138. — Traces the development of differential psychology from a loosely joined bundle of topics, through an integrated field of psychology, to a distinct orientation toward all psychology. The differential orientation is characterized by (1) the recognition and measurement of variability as a fundamental property of all behavior and (2) the comparative analysis of behavior under varying environmental and biological conditions, as 1 approach to understanding the nature and sources of behavior. Major orienting concepts that can be widely applied within general psychology include the multiplicity and interaction of variables involved in behavioral effects, the overlapping of distributions, the multidimensionality of individual and group differences, and the development of individuality in relation to multiple group membership. (German abstract)

29177. **Spiegelman, J. Marvin. Judaism and Jungian psychology.** University Press of America: Lanham, MD, 1993. xi, 156 pp. ISBN 0-8191-8895-6 (hardcover).
**TABLE OF CONTENTS**
Introduction • Part I: Harmony • Jewish psycho-ecumenism (Univ. of Judaism, 1989) • A Jewish psychotherapist looks at the religious function of the psyche (Association of Orthodox Jewish Scientists, UCLA, 1989) • Struggling with the image of God (Cedars-Sinai Conference on Psychology and Judaism 1986) • Judaism and Jungian psychology: A personal experience • Part II: Disharmony • The Jewish understanding of evil in the light of Jung's psychology (1988) • Part III: Harmony and disharmony together • Julia, the atheist-communist • The medium, Sophie-Sarah
*[from the publicity materials]* There has been a significant amount of commentary about the Jung who was, on the one hand, thought to harbor anti-Semitic sentiment and, on the other hand, a friend and teacher of many Jews. His school of psychology has had a large Jewish following throughout the world, including Israel. J. Marvin Spiegelman uses the works of C. G. Jung to foster a dialogue between Judaism and Christianity. He demonstrates the parallels between Jung's thought and classic Kabbalistic views on the masculine and feminine aspects of Divinity and all life; "Judaism and Jungian Psychology" supplements the work of Martin

Buber and Eric Fromm in this area of Biblical research. Spiegelman includes some of his own fiction, psychomythological in theme, from "The Tree."

29291. **Foster, Susan E. & Brizius, Jack A.** (Brizius & Foster, Private Consultant). **Caring too much? American women and the nation's caregiving crisis.** [In: (PA Vol 80:29128) *Women on the front lines: Meeting the challenge of an aging America.* Allen, Jessie & Pifer, Alan (Eds.). Urban Institute Press: Washington, DC, 1993. xv. 270 pp. ISBN 0-87766-574-5 (hardcover); 0-87766-575-3 (paperback).] pp. 47–73.
*[from the chapter]*
— as America's caregivers, women hold the family together and maintain the social structure of the country ◊ the combination of increased survival rates, lower mortality at very old ages, and women's increased labor force participation means that caregiving is no longer a potentially satisfying, if burdensome, way of life but, instead, a crisis for an expanding proportion of women in America ◊ explores the dimensions of that crisis and examines ways in which public policy might be formulated to alleviate at least part of the burden of caregiving, which is sure to increase in the near future as our population ages.

31608. **Draper, Elaine.** (U Southern California, Los Angeles) **Fetal exclusion policies and gendered constructions of suitable work.** Special Issue: Environmental justice. *Social Problems,* 1993(Feb), Vol 40(1), 90–107. —Examines fetal exclusion policies (FEPs) and argues against employers' claims that scientific research supports their definition of unacceptable risk used to exclude women from jobs requiring exposure to toxic substances. Definitions of acceptable risk in FEPs are not scientific or value-neutral, but are in fact socially constructed, and therefore reflect gender stratification, corporate control, and the culturally privileged position of the fetus. This is evident in 3 of these policies' effects: (1) They exclude only certain fertile women, not all workers at risk; (2) they give priority to fetal rights, at the expense of workers' rights; and (3) corporations see them as the least costly defense against damage suits. Also examined is problematic free choice rhetoric pervading the US Supreme Court case regarding the Johnson Controls Corporation's FEP. Conceptions and power relationships that underlie fetal exclusion are also discussed.

material supplied by the publisher. It also shows the name and location of the publisher, the copyright date, the number of prefatory pages, the length of the book, and a unique code assigned by the publisher that identifies this edition of the book (the ISBN, or International Standard Book Number). The abstract of the chapter by Foster and Brizius contains parenthetical information about the book in which it appeared and notes that the book was previously indexed in *Psychological Abstracts*. Open diamonds (◊) are used to separate a quoted phrase.

If you were doing a literature search on a topic in education, another useful resource would be ERIC (Educational Resources Information Center), an abstract service that is funded by the U.S. Department of Education. Exhibit 7 shows an annotated ERIC abstract of a document; similar abstracts can be found in *Resources in Education* (*RIE*). Exhibit 8 shows an annotated ERIC abstract of a journal article; these abstracts can be found in *Current Index to Journals in Education* (*CIJE*).

Other useful abstract services in psychology, education, and related areas include *Sociological Abstracts* (1952 to present) and the often overlooked *Social Sciences Index* (1974 to present). There are abstracts and indexes for just about every discipline and area of interest (for example, *Biological Abstracts*, *Art Index*, *Abridged Index Medicus*, and *Humanities Index*), and a librarian will be glad to direct you to the relevant indexes and abstracts. *Psychological Abstracts* (and most other indexes) include an author index and a subject index. The subject index is valuable if used with care. Avoid looking up a broad topic that will have pages of listings; for instance, to find material on the learning abilities of insects, check *insects*, not *learning*. (If you would like to have a comprehensive list of relevant indexes and abstracts, see "Bibliographical Retrieval for the Social and Behavioral Scientist," by MaryLu C. Rosenthal, *Research in Higher Education*, 1985, vol. 22, pp. 315–333.)

## Using PsycLIT

A computer search is usually faster and more fun than a hand search, and using a machine is really the only way to begin an exhaustive search on a given topic. If you are using PsycLIT (which covers 1974 to the present), begin by asking a librarian whether you can obtain a copy of the *PsycLIT Quick Reference Guide*; it defines symbols and commands and will lead you step by step through

**EXHIBIT 7** ERIC document abstract from *Resources in Education**

---

**ERIC Accession Number**—identification number sequentially assigned to documents as they are processed.

**Author(s)**

**Title**

**Institution.** (Organization where document originated.)

**Date Published**

**Contract or Grant Number**

**Language of Document**—documents written entirely in English are not designated, although "English" is carried in their computerized records.

**Publication Type**—broad categories indicating the form or organization of the document, as contrasted to its subject matter. The category name is followed by the category code.

**ERIC Document Reproduction Service (EDRS) Availability**— "MF" means microfiche; "PC" means reproduced paper copy. When described as "Document Not Available from EDRS," alternate sources are cited above. Prices are subject to change; for latest price code schedule see section on "How to Order ERIC Documents," in the most recent issue of RIE.

**Abstractor's Initials**

---

**Clearinghouse Accession Number**

**Sponsoring Agency**—agency responsible for initiating, funding, and managing the research project.

**Report Number**— assigned by originator.

**Descriptive Note** (pagination first).

**Alternate source for obtaining document**

**Journal Citation**

**Descriptors**—subject terms found in the *Thesaurus of ERIC Descriptors* that characterize substantive content. Only the major terms (preceded by an asterisk) are printed in the Subject Index.

**Identifiers**—additional identifying terms not found in the *Thesaurus*. Only the major terms (preceded by an asterisk) are printed in the Subject Index.

**Informative Abstract**

---

ED 654 321        CE 123 456
*Butler, Kathleen*      *Smith, B. James*
**Career Planning for Women.**
Central Univ., Chicago, IL.
Spons Agency — Office of Educational Research and Improvement (ED), Washington, DC.
Report No. — ISBN-0-3333-5568-1; OERI-91-34
Pub Date — May 92
Contract — RI900000
Note — 30p.; An abridged version of this report was presented at the National Conference on Educational Opportunities for Women (9th, Chicago, IL, May 14-16, 1992).
Available from — Campus Bookstore, 123 College Avenue, Chicago, IL 60690 ($5.95).
Language — English, Spanish
Journal Cit—Women Today; v13 n3 p1-14 Jan 1992
Pub Type— Reports—Descriptive (141)—Tests/Questionnaires (160)
**EDRS Price—MF01/PC02 Plus Postage.**
Descriptors — Career Guidance, *Career Planning, *Demand Occupations, *Employed Women, *Employment Opportunities, Females, Labor Force, Labor Market, Postsecondary Education
Identifiers — Consortium of States, *National Occupational Competency Testing Institute
Women's opportunities for employment will be directly related to their level of skill and experience and also to the labor market demands through the remainder of the decade. The number of workers needed for all major occupational categories is expected to increase by about one-fifth between 1990 and 1999, but the growth rate will vary by occupational group. Professional and technical workers are expected to have the highest predicted rate (39 percent), followed by service workers (35 percent), clerical workers (26 percent), sales workers (24 percent), craft workers and supervisors (20 percent), managers and administrators (15 percent), and operatives (11 percent). This publication contains a brief discussion and employment information (in English and in Spanish) concerning occupations for professional and technical workers, managers and administrators, skilled trades, sales workers, clerical workers, and service workers. In order for women to take advantage of increased labor market demands, employer attitudes toward working women need to change and women must: (1) receive better career planning and counseling, (2) change their career aspirations, and (3) fully utilize the sources of legal protection and assistance that are available to them. (Contains 45 references.)
(SB)

---

*Reproduced by permission of the Director of the ERIC Facility, U.S. Department of Education.

**EXHIBIT 8**   ERIC journal article abstract from *Current Index to Journals in Education**

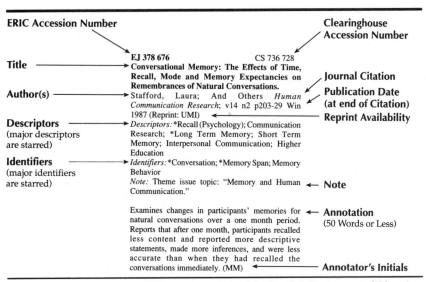

**ERIC Accession Number**

**Clearinghouse Accession Number**

EJ 378 676                              CS 736 728

**Title** — Conversational Memory: The Effects of Time, Recall, Mode and Memory Expectancies on Remembrances of Natural Conversations.

**Journal Citation**

**Author(s)** — Stafford, Laura; And Others *Human Communication Research*; v14 n2 p203-29 Win 1987 (Reprint: UMI)

**Publication Date (at end of Citation)**

**Reprint Availability**

**Descriptors** (major descriptors are starred) — *Descriptors:*\*Recall (Psychology); Communication Research; \*Long Term Memory; Short Term Memory; Interpersonal Communication; Higher Education

**Identifiers** (major identifiers are starred) — *Identifiers:*\*Conversation; \*Memory Span; Memory Behavior

*Note:* Theme issue topic: "Memory and Human Communication." — **Note**

Examines changes in participants' memories for natural conversations over a one month period. Reports that after one month, participants recalled less content and reported more descriptive statements, made more inferences, and were less accurate than when they had recalled the conversations immediately. (MM) — **Annotation** (50 Words or Less)

**Annotator's Initials**

*Reproduced by permission of the Director of the ERIC Facility, U.S. Department of Education.

some basic search techniques. However, you will find that PsycLIT also contains its own on-screen tutorial to show you how to conduct a search. Press the "Ctrl" and "t" keys simultaneously to "boot" (start up) the tutorial. Once you have the system booted, you can press the "F1" key to get any general help you need. You will find the system user-friendly and also time-saving if you do some homework on the topic before you actually get going. Looking in the APA's *Thesaurus of Psychological Index Terms* can save you a lot of time and effort. This handy resource contains the vocabulary (words and phrases) used to index *Psychological Abstracts*, so you can avoid the problem of creating search terms that are not used to index materials. You can also summon the thesaurus by pressing the "F9" key once you are into PsycLIT.

Donna Shires (a doctoral student and teaching fellow at Temple University) recently had this to say based on her experience using PsycLIT:

> I was writing a paper about how questionnaire results may be biased by the way the questions themselves are worded. Specifically, I was interested in the problem of people answering "yes" to questions that they might not really agree with. My understanding was that this problem was called *yea-saying*. Armed

with this limited knowledge, I got on PsycLIT and entered the term *yea-saying*. I found only two articles that addressed this topic. Because my paper required a literature review, I became a little worried. Two articles could hardly be considered a literature review. At this point, I decided to go back to some textbooks that had information on questionnaire design. Upon reading more information, I discovered that the term *yea-saying* was not the most general or common term for the problem I was interested in. Rather, *acquiescent response bias*, or some variation thereof, was the term of choice. When I got back on PsycLIT and plugged in *acquiescent*, I found a whole list of articles. My literature review could proceed!

Donna ran into the opposite problem in another situation, when she turned up many articles that were not relevant to what she wanted:

I was interested in finding studies that had looked at people's attitudes toward the mentally ill. I used the terms *attitude,\** *mentally,* and *ill* in this search. When I combined these (by first combining *mentally* and *ill* and then adding *attitude\**), PsycLIT informed me that more than 70 articles contained these terms. In looking these articles over, I found that some had to do with attitudes *of* mentally ill people, not attitudes *about* mentally ill people. When I used the terms *mental* and *illness* with *attitude\**, I located articles that dealt with attitudes *about* the mentally ill.

Donna prepares her own students with the following background information and hints:

➤ Actually using PsycLIT requires that you understand what it is capable of doing for you. It locates articles in psychology journals and journals in related fields. These articles are located based on the term(s) you tell PsycLIT to search for. At the "Find" prompt, you type in the term that you want to use as the basis of your search. PsycLIT will then conduct a search, assign the search a number, tell you how many articles contain the term, and give you the option of looking at the citation and abstract for each of these articles.

➤ The PsycLIT search process can be speeded up and simplified if you know a few tricks. One of these is to search for only one term at a time; this means, generally, one word at a time. Let's say you want to find information on racial prejudice. The fastest way to do this search is first to type in *racial* at the "Find" prompt. Once this search has been completed, tell PsycLIT to find *prejudice*. Following this search, tell PsycLIT to find "#1 and #2" (or whatever the assigned numbers are). This approach works more efficiently than typing in *racial prejudice* as one term. Also, separating your search into specific words can save you time later on. For example, let's say that you think that racial prejudice may be related to stereotyping. You do a search on *stereotype*, which is assigned the number 5. You can then command PsycLIT to find "#1 and #5" to see what articles are available on racial stereotypes.

➤ Another hint has to do with how you spell the term you are searching for. When searching the literature for articles on acquiescent responding, Donna found that some authors referred to this problem as *acquiescent response bias* and others used the term *acquiescence*. Rather than conducting several searches using each variation, she typed *acquiescen\** at the "Find" prompt. In this way, she told PsycLIT to search for that particular term and allowed for several different endings to the term. Therefore, articles using both *acquiescent* and *acquiescence* came up in the search.

➤ The number of articles you locate can give you information on whether you are too narrow or too broad in your search. If your search locates no articles, you are probably using the wrong term. If you locate only one or two articles, you may be searching for something too specific or using the wrong term. If a search turns up large numbers of articles, you may need to narrow down your topic. If you have your own personal computer with a floppy drive, you can download information from PsycLIT and look it over at your convenience, so you can deal with large numbers of articles. However, you may also want to add a term to narrow the search. For example, if you are interested in the treatment of depression, you can specify particular types of treatment to get the number of articles down to a reasonable size.

When it is time to print, download, or both, Donna prepares her students with the following hints:

➤ You will find it useful to have the complete abstract of the article as well as the citation. PsycLIT's default option is citation only, which then prints the titles of all articles located in the search. You will need to change "CITN" to "ALL" to get the full abstract.

➤ To get only specific articles, enter the code number assigned to these articles by PsycLIT. Articles are arranged chronologically, with the most recently published ones listed first.

➤ If you are printing out directly from the PsycLIT database to a printer, it is generally better to look over the articles and print only those that are relevant. This gives you more time to conduct searches, because most printers are not very fast.

➤ If downloading to a floppy disk, you may just want to download all articles and look them over later. This saves the most time. However, make sure that you get the full abstract when you download, because just the article citation tells you little.

## Ordering a Literature Search

If your library charges to do a literature search for you, begin by talking with a staff member who can help you choose the key words and descriptors that will facilitate your retrieval of the desired literature and will exclude scores of irrelevant citations. You will be asked to pare down your topic as precisely as you can and to avoid undertaking a complete search on a broad topic. For example, if you ask for material on "social behavior in children," you will probably get an unmanageable printout and a big bill. As in painting a room or blacktopping a driveway, the more effort and thought spent in conscientious preparation for the task, the better the final outcome.

Be prepared to consider the following points when you approach the staff member to place your order:

➤ What is the particular topic to be searched? In answering this question, use special terms as well as common words, including synonyms and alternate spellings. Answer the question as fully as possible, and define any words or phrases you use that may have special meaning within your area of interest.

➤ Describe any related terms or applications in which you are *not* interested, so the computer can be instructed to discard seemingly relevant but actually inappropriate references. This consideration will help reduce the cost of your search. The APA's *Thesaurus of Psychological Index Terms* can help you pare down the search.

➤ List two or three of the most important authors on your topic. This list, plus the following three points, will help the computer zero in on your topic.

➤ List two or three of the most important journals in your subject.

➤ List two or three of the most significant articles on your topic. If you do not know enough about your subject to make such a list, ask your instructor for suggestions, or check current reference books or standard textbooks for clues.

➤ Give the time span that you would like the search to cover. *Psychological Abstracts* covers the period from 1927 to the present, and PsycINFO (the online system) covers 1967 to the present. The time spans of indexes and abstracts vary widely; the librarian will tell you the years covered by the databases to which your library subscribes.

# The Fugitive Literature

Work that is unpublished or simply hard to find is termed the **fugitive literature.** For example, private institutions and government agencies support research that may be circulated only in technical reports. Other examples of the fugitive literature include papers that researchers present at professional meetings, as well as dissertations and theses that graduate students write. If the work you are seeking is in the interlibrary loan network, you can request that your library borrow it for you.

There are specific ways to track down fugitive literature. For example, if you are familiar with an author's previous work, you can write to that person for follow-up studies, talks, technical reports, and so on. You will increase the likelihood of obtaining a response if your request is precise and convincing. Researchers receive many requests for reprints, preprints, and other information, so do not expect a busy researcher to answer a long list of questions or to send you material that is readily available in any college library.

If you are in a department that has many active researchers on the staff, it is possible that one of them is working on the very problem in which you are interested. If so, set up an appointment to discuss your interests, but be sure to do your homework on the subject first. List for yourself the questions you want to ask, and then take notes during the interview.

A database called NTIS (National Technical Information Service) makes available summaries of completed research (including conference proceedings and theses) in the United States and abroad. Your library may also have catalogs of government publications. For information about theses and dissertations, see *Dissertation Abstracts International*, *Masters Abstracts*, *Research Abstracts*, and *American Doctoral Dissertations*.

## Other Resources

Suppose you come across a word or phrase that you do not understand and cannot find in your desk dictionary or in the library's unabridged dictionaries. If it is a psychological term, you can try to find it in other reference works, such as the psychological or educational encyclopedias noted previously. The best unabridged dictionary of the English language is the multivolume *Oxford English Dictionary (OED)*, which is fascinating to thumb through if you are interested in word origins. Its purpose is to give the history of all words in the English language from the year A.D. 1150 to the publication of the *OED*. There is an abridged edition in two volumes (also published by the Oxford University Press), but you need a magnifying glass to read it. Some words in the *OED* have very different meanings today than they had originally, and it can be fun to learn about these changes in meaning.

A great many other useful dictionaries and reference sources are available. For example, slang dictionaries will tell you the history of words such as *hot dog* and *meathead*. They also provide information on rhyming slang, black slang, pig Latin, and so forth. If you are interested in information about people in the news, you can look in *Current Biography*. If you want to know about famous Americans from the past, you can look in the *Dictionary of American Biography* or *Who Was Who in America*. The *Dictionary of National Biography* tells about men and women in British history. Librarians can point you to other works that you may find useful.

## Taking Notes in the Library

We have discussed locating material but not taking notes in the library. You need to take precise, carefully documented background notes to write an accurate paper. Detailed notes not only help you pull facts and ideas together into precise sentences and paragraphs but also help you avoid committing *plagiarism* accidentally. We will have more to say about plagiarism in Chapter 5, but you plagiarize intentionally when you knowingly copy or summarize someone's work without acknowledging that source. You plagiarize accidentally when you copy someone's work but forget to credit it or to put it in quotation marks. Plagiarism is illegal, and you should guard against it by taking accurate notes.

A good procedure for taking notes in the library is to use a separate index card for each quotable idea that you find as you uncover relevant material in your literature search. Many writers prefer making notes on 5 × 8-inch index cards because they can usually get all the information they want on the front of a large card, so it's easier to find what they want later. Exhibit 9 shows two examples of notes taken for a term paper; the student found two sections in one source for use in the paper.

Observe that the cards are numbered "1 of 2" and "2 of 2" in the upper-right corner, and the book's call number is included at the lower left. If you have made an outline for a term paper (as described in Chapter 3), you might code each card (in the lower right) with the particular section of the outline that the material on the card will illustrate (or you may color-code your cards). In this way you can maintain a general order in your notes and avoid facing a huge stack of miscellaneous bits and pieces of information that will loom large as you try to sort and integrate the information you find in the library into a useful form. Be consistent with all the reference numbers you use on your note cards; a haphazard arrangement will only slow you down when it is time to write the first draft.

The two index cards in Exhibit 9 contain a wealth of material. At the top of both cards is a complete citation. Such a citation will be required in your reference section (where you list all the sources you have cited) and will be condensed in the citations in the paper's

**EXHIBIT 9** Sample note cards

Rosenthal, Robert, and Jacobson, Lenore (1968). *Pygmalion in the classroom: Teacher expectation and pupils' intellectual development.* New York: Holt, Rinehart and Winston

1 of 2

Teachers at "Oak School" (an elementary school in California) were led to believe that about 20% of students were potential "bloomers" based on their performance on a test to pick out intellectual bloomers (or spurters). Actually, the names of the 20% had been chosen at random and the test was a nonverbal IQ test (TOGA). All students were retested with TOGA after one semester, after a full academic year, and after two academic years. The IQ gains of the 20% (the experimental group) consistently surpassed the IQ gains of the remaining (control group) students. This result is consistent with Rosenthal's self-fulfilling prophecy hypothesis (see also Merton, R.). The authors conclude that "... one person's expectation for another person's behavior can quite unwittingly become a more accurate prediction simply for its having been made." (page vii)

LB1131.R585

Rosenthal, Robert, and Jacobson, Lenore (1968). *Pygmalion in the classroom: Teacher expectation and pupils' intellectual development.* New York: Holt, Rinehart and Winston.

2 of 2

What practical implications do these authors draw from their research findings? "As teacher-training institutions begin to teach the possibility that teachers' expectations of their pupils' performance may serve as self-fulfilling prophecies, there may be a new expectancy created. The new expectancy may be that children can learn more than had been believed possible, an expectation held by many educational theorists, though for quite different reasons.... The new expectancy, at the very least, will make it more difficult when they encounter the educationally disadvantaged for teachers to think, 'Well, after all, what can you expect?' The man on the street may be permitted his opinions and prophecies of the unkempt children loitering in a dreary schoolyard. The teacher in the schoolroom may need to learn that those same prophecies within her may be fulfilled; she is no casual passer-by. Perhaps Pygmalion in the classroom is more her role." (pp. 181–182)

LB1131.R585

narrative. The top card summarizes, in the notetaker's own words, the major details of the study reported by Rosenthal and Jacobson. This synopsis ends with a quotation chosen to illustrate Rosenthal and Jacobson's conclusions. Note that the page number of the quote is included; the page number must be cited if the student decides to use this quote. On the bottom card the student has focused the material taken from this book by asking a particular question. The lengthy quotation copied from Rosenthal and Jacobson specifically addresses the question. Notice that four dots (a period plus an ellipsis) interrupt the text halfway through the quote; they indicate that a portion of the quote has been purposely omitted by the student.

The most fundamental rule is to be thorough and systematic so you do not waste time and energy having to run back to the same book or article. Because memory is porous, it is better to write down too much than to rely on recall to fill in the gaps. Be sure your notes will make sense to you when you examine them later.

## Additional Tips

Here are some more tips to help you get started on the literature search:

> Try to be realistic in assessing how many books and articles you will need in your literature review. Too few may result in a weak foundation for your project, but too much material and intemperate expectations can overwhelm you and your subject. You are not writing a doctoral dissertation or an article for publication but a paper that must be completed within a limited time frame.

> How can you find out what is a happy medium between too little and too much? Talk with your instructor before you start an intensive literature search. Ask whether your plan seems realistic.

> Before you begin your literature search, ask the instructor to recommend any key works that you should read or consult. Even if you feel confident about your topic already, asking the instructor for specific leads can prevent you from going off on a tangent.

> Do not expect to finish your literature search in one sitting. Students with unrealistic expectations make themselves overly anxious and rush a task that should

be done patiently and methodically to achieve the best result.

➤ In planning your schedule, give yourself ample time to do a thorough job. Patience will pay off by making you feel more confident that you understand your topic well.

➤ It is not always easy to discard a study that you have made an effort to track down, but quantity should not replace quality and relevance in the studies you finally use in your research report or term paper. Your instructor will be more impressed by a tightly reasoned paper than by one overflowing with superfluous background material.

➤ Suppose you cannot locate the original work that you are looking for in the stacks. Some students return repeatedly to the library, day after day, seeking a book or journal article before discovering that it has been lost or stolen or is being rebound. Ask an information librarian to find the elusive material. If the original work you need is unavailable, the librarian may consult another college library.

➤ If you are looking for a specialized work, you probably will not find it in a small public library, so do not waste your time. When students spend a lot of time off-campus in public libraries and bookstores looking for source material, they usually come back with references from general texts or current mass-market books and periodicals.

## Library Etiquette

Before we turn to the basics of outlining the term paper (Chapter 3) or structuring the research report (Chapter 4), here is some final advice about using the library. The golden rule of library etiquette is to treat others as you would have them treat you, which means:

➤ Be quiet while working in the library.
➤ Never tear out pages of journals or books.
➤ Never write in library journals and books.
➤ Do not monopolize material.
➤ Return books and periodicals as soon as you finish with them.

# CHAPTER THREE

# Outlining the Term Paper

*Once you have chosen your topic and begun library work and note taking, the next step in developing the term paper is to make an outline. The imposition of form will help you collect and refine your thoughts as you shape the paper. (If you are writing a research report, you can skip this chapter and go on to Chapter 4.)*

## Where to Start

Instructors are usually very sensitive to a weak structure or lack of structure in term papers because they have to read so many of them. When you outline your paper before you begin writing it, you are making a "road map" to the ideas and notes that you are assembling to present in your paper. If done correctly, the outline will show a logical progression of the points of interest that the paper will cover. Initially, you can generate a tentative and general outline as you use the library's resources to search for reference material to flesh out the paper when the time comes to sit down and write.

If you find it difficult to begin making an outline, there are several tricks you can try. One is to shop around for an interesting quote that encourages fresh thinking and can later launch the introduction as well as capture and focus the reader's interest. A second trick to help you get started is to ask yourself the reporter's questions: *who, what, when, where,* and *why.* A third trick is to use comparison and contrast as a way of structuring the outline in your mind; then pull together specific facts and studies to document and expand on your subtopics.

Before you begin writing (discussed in Chapter 5), you will want to revise the preliminary outline so that it reflects the organizational structure you will use to shape the paper.

## Making Ideas Parallel

Outline items can be set down in three different forms: topics, sentences, or paragraphs. The specific form chosen should be the only one used in the outline so that all the ideas are parallel. In the following outline fragment, based on Maria's paper in Appendix A, the ideas are clearly not parallel:

I. Nature of problem
   A. Food plentiful but eating disorder results
   B. How is it defined?
   C. Symptoms
      1. Weight loss
      2. Patient has a distorted body image
   D. Psychological aspects of the disorder include:
      1. Perfectionist's disease
      2. See themselves as obese

The problem with this outline is that it is a hodgepodge of topics, idea fragments, questions, and so forth. Working with this jumble is like swimming upstream. Such an outline will only sabotage your efforts to put thoughts and notes into a logical sequence. Contrast this inconsistent structure with the parallel structure of the following outline as it covers the same points:

I. Nature of the problem
   A. Food plentiful, but eating disorder is widespread
   B. Definition
      1. A.n. defined by Dorland's (p. 94) as "a serious nervous condition in which the patient loses his appetite and systematically takes but little food, so that he becomes greatly emaciated."
      2. *Anorexia* from Greek "want of appetite"
      3. *Nervosa,* a nervous condition

C. Symptoms
1. Emaciation
2. Depression
3. Distorted body image
4. Refusal to maintain normal weight

# Putting Ideas in Order

Whether you use topics, sentences, or paragraphs for your outline, group your information in descending order from the most general facts or ideas to the most specific details and examples. We see this approach clearly in the parallel format of the outline shown immediately above. As the following example illustrates, the same rule applies whether you are outlining definitions and symptoms or the nature of a specific therapeutic approach in a clinical investigation that you plan to develop further in the first draft:

II. Symptom-oriented approach
A. Behavior therapy
1. Early example (Bachrach et al., 1965)
2. 14-year follow-up (Erwin, 1977)
3. No beneficial effect found (Eckert et al., 1979)
4. Use of systematic desensitization (Lang, 1965)
5. Critique
a. Effect short-lived (Bruch, 1979)
b. Deprivation of privileges (Bemis, 1978)
c. Small N's (Eckert et al., 1979)
d. Confounding by medications (Eckert et al., 1979)
B. Organic procedures
1. Lithium carbonate (Gross et al., 1980)
a. Ignores psychological factors (Andersen, 1979; Bemis, 1978)
b. Can produce physical problems (Mitchell & Eckert, 1987)
2. Amitriptyline (antidepressant) (Mitchell & Eckert, 1987)
a. Used with bulimic anorexics (Halmi et al., 1986)
b. Higher pretreatment depression
c. Limited use recommended (Andersen, 1987)

**EXHIBIT 10** Subdivision of the outline

---

I.
  A.
  B.
    1.
    2.
      a.
      b.
        (1)
        (2)
          (a)
          (b)
II.
  A.
  B.

---

3. Cyproheptadine (antihistaminic, antipruritic) (Goldberg et al., 1979; Halmi et al., 1986)
   a. More weight gain among anorexics with previous treatment failures and history of complications at birth (Goldberg et al., 1979)
   b. Anorexics without bulimia benefit most (Halmi et al., 1986)
   c. Differences in treatment effectiveness found in different hospitals (Halmi et al., 1986)

Another convention in making an outline is that there should be two or more subtopics under any topic, as illustrated in Exhibit 10. The use of roman numerals I, II, III; capitals A, B, C; arabic numerals 1, 2, 3; small letters a, b, c; and finally numbers and letters in parentheses serves as a means of classifying facts, ideas, and concepts. Thus, if you list I, you should list II; if A, then B; if 1, then 2; and so on.

The roman numerals indicate the outline's main ideas. Indented capital letters provide main divisions within each main idea. The letters and numbers that follow list the supporting details and examples. Note the indentation of each subtopic. Any category can be expanded to fit the number of supporting details or examples that you wish to cover in the paper. Any lapses in logic are bound to surface if you use this system of organization, and you can catch and correct them before proceeding.

For example, look at the following abbreviated outline; the entry labeled "B" is a conspicuous lapse in logic:

I. Symptoms
    A. Weight loss
    B. Use psychotherapy for patient
    C. Distorted body image

Item B should be moved from this section of the outline to that pertaining to therapeutic approaches. Another instance might require a return to the library to clarify a point or to fill in with the appropriate reference material.

## Further Helpful Hints

The outline is a way not only to organize your thoughts but also to make it easier to start writing. If you use the phrase or sentence format, the paper will almost write itself. We see this clearly by returning to the outline of the opening section in Maria's paper:

I. Nature of the problem
    A. Food plentiful, but eating disorder is widespread
    B. Definition
        1. A.n. defined by Dorland's (p. 94) as "a serious nervous condition in which the patient loses his appetite and systematically takes but little food, so that he becomes greatly emaciated."
        2. *Anorexia* from Greek "want of appetite"
        3. *Nervosa*, a nervous condition

Had the outline used complete sentences, the opening paragraph of Maria's paper would write itself:

I. Nature of the problem
    A. In a society where food is plentiful and a topic of obsessive attention, it is paradoxical that anorexia can be so prevalent.
        1. Dorland's (p. 94) defines *anorexia nervosa* as "a serious nervous condition in which the patient loses his appetite and systematically takes but little food, so that he becomes greatly emaciated."

2. *Anorexia* is from the Greek "want of appetite."
3. *Nervosa* indicates a nervous condition.
B. Distorted self-image is one basic symptom, as victims starve themselves to achieve weight loss because they misperceive themselves as layered in fat.

In Chapter 2 we alluded to one other helpful hint about using an outline. The outline's coding system makes it convenient to code the notes you take during your literature search in the library. If the notes on an index card pertain to section "II.B.1." of your outline, then you would write this code on the card. In this way, order is brought to the stack of note cards that you accumulate. If you spread them out on a table and sort them according to the section of the outline they pertain to, the paper will take shape from your notes and the outline, each component enhancing the other.

Keep in mind, however, that the outline is only a guide. Its form will probably change as you integrate your notes and your outline.

## Outlining After the Fact

Some people find the process of making an outline too exacting, preferring instead to sit at a word processor, at a typewriter, or with pencil and pad so that the stream of ideas can flow spontaneously. An experienced writer working with a familiar topic sometimes achieves success with this unstructured approach. But for others, the results often create havoc and frustration, not to mention wasted time and effort.

If you feel that you do not have the self-discipline to make an outline at the outset, then at least make one later. To assure yourself that your work has an appealing, coherent form—what psychologists call a *good Gestalt*—see if you can outline your first draft after the fact if you did not make an outline beforehand. Ask yourself:

➤ Is the discussion focused, and do the ideas flow from or build on one another?
➤ Is there ample development of each idea?
➤ Are there supporting details for each main idea discussed?
➤ Are the ideas balanced?
➤ Is the writing to the point, or have I gone off on a tangent?

If you would like to practice on someone else's work, try out-lining the section "Context-Oriented Approach" in Maria's paper. Ask yourself how well her discussion addresses the five preceding questions. If you find problems with the structure of her discus-sion, think of ways she could have avoided them or corrected them after the first draft.

# CHAPTER FOUR

# Planning the Research Report

*The research report has a structure in which data form its core. The literature review usually involves only a few key studies. This chapter describes the structure and form of the research report and suggests ways to begin organizing your thoughts. (If you are writing a term paper, then you can skip this chapter and go on to Chapter 5.)*

## The Basic Structure

By now, course work and your instructor's recommendations should have led you through the process of narrowing your area of interest so that your study is feasible and ethical and your methods and procedures are appropriate to it. Many texts on research methods routinely cover data collection and data analysis. We will assume that you are mastering the relevant techniques they describe, so what remains is to plan a clear, concise report.

Notice that John's research report has eight parts:

- Title Page
- Abstract
- Introduction
- Method
- Results
- Discussion
- References
- Appendix

Except for the layout of the title page and the addition of the appendix, the structure of this report corresponds to the standard format that has evolved over many years. The title page is straightforward, so we will focus on the remaining seven parts of the research report.

# Abstract

Although the abstract appears at the beginning of your report, it is actually written after you complete the rest of your paper. The abstract provides a concise summary of your report. Think of it as a distillation of the important points covered in the body of the report. Thus, in one succinct paragraph in the sample research report, John gives a synopsis of his hypothesis, the methodology of the investigation, and his results.

When planning your abstract, answer these questions as concisely as possible:

➤ What was the objective or purpose of my research study?
➤ What principal method did I use?
➤ Who were the research participants?
➤ What were my major findings?
➤ What can I conclude from these findings?

More-detailed and more-specific statements about methods, results, and conclusions are treated in the body of your report. The brief summary of the abstract lets the reader anticipate what your report is about.

# Introduction

The introduction to the report should give a concise history and background of your topic. In the sample report, John quotes a classic poem to support his claim that interest in rumor goes far back in history. He then defines the term that forms the basis of his study and delves into the current status of the topic. In this way, the reader is given some general facts needed to appreciate and assess John's work. He cites specific studies to provide the reader with additional background on the topic and then raises a question ("Why are some rumors repeated more frequently than others?") that allows him to lead into his hypothesis in an inviting way.

The introduction provides the rationale for your study and prepares the reader for the methods you have chosen. The literature review shows the development of your hypothesis and the reason you believe the research question to be important. The strongest introductions are those that state the research problem or the hypothesis posed in such a way that the method section appears to be a natural consequence of that statement. If you can get readers to think when they later see your method section, "Yes, of course, that's what this researcher had to do to answer this question," then you will have succeeded in writing a strong introduction.

Here are some questions to ask yourself as you plan the introduction:

➤ What was the purpose of my study?
➤ What terms need to be defined?
➤ How does my study build on or derive from other studies?
➤ What was my working hypothesis or expectation?

# Method

The next step is to detail exactly the methods and procedures used. Care should be taken to describe fully the research participant pool: the age, sex, and numbers of subjects, as well as the way in which they were selected and any other details that would help to specify them. Psychologists are trained to ask questions about the generalizability of research findings. Your psychology instructor will be thinking about the generalizability of your results across both persons and settings (that is, the **external validity** of the results).

If you recruited participants from an available subject pool, it would be informative to tell how many of the potential subjects actually volunteered. If you happen to know something about the characteristics of the subjects who did not volunteer (that is, the nonrespondents), you might wish to report this information as well (perhaps in a table that compares the characteristics of the respondents and the nonrespondents). *The Volunteer Subject* (Wiley, 1975), by Robert Rosenthal and Ralph L. Rosnow, will help you explain the ways in which external validity may be affected by the subjects' volunteer status.

Also included in this section should be a description of the tests and measurements that you chose to use and the context in which they were presented. John's report describes the brief questionnaire that he prepared and the instructions given to the participants. He notes that the participants were aware they were responding anonymously; it is believed that people respond more candidly and honestly when the anonymity or confidentiality of their responses can be guaranteed. For a recent discussion of this issue, see "Scientific Rewards and Conflicts of Ethical Choices in Human Subjects Research," by Peter David Blanck and others, which appeared in the *American Psychologist* in 1992 (vol. 47, pp. 959–965).

Even if you used well-known, standardized tests (TAT, MMPI, or WAIS, for example), it is still a good idea to capsulize them in a few sentences. By describing them, you communicate to the reader that you understand the nature and purpose of the tests you chose. Suppose you used the Self-Monitoring Scale developed by Mark Snyder (see "Self Monitoring of Expressive Behavior," by Mark Snyder, *Journal of Personality and Social Psychology*, 1974, vol. 30, pp. 526–537). If you did a literature search, as described in Chapter 2, you would learn that follow-up research by other investigators found that this scale consists of three different dimensions (see "An Analysis of the Self-Monitoring Scale," by S. R. Briggs, J. M. Cheek, and A. H. Buss, *Journal of Personality and Social Psychology*, 1980, vol. 38, pp. 679–686).

Knowing this background information, you could describe the instrument you used as follows:

> Subjects were presented with Snyder's (1974) 25-item Self-Monitoring Scale, which was designed to measure the extent of self-observation and self-control guided by situational cues to social appropriateness. Briggs, Cheek, and Buss (1980) showed the multidimensional nature of this test, identifying three distinct factors that form internally consistent subscales. The Extraversion Subscale was described by Briggs et al. as tapping the respondent's chronic tendency to be the center of attention in groups, to tell stories and jokes, and so on. The Other-Directedness Subscale was described as measuring the respondent's willingness to change his or her behavior to suit others. The Acting Subscale was described as assessing liking and being good at speaking and entertaining.

However, suppose you needed to report only the nature of a particular test and not any follow-up inferences by other researchers. Let us say the test was John T. Cacioppo and Richard E. Petty's Need for Cognition Scale (see "The Need for Cognition," by J. T. Cacioppo and R. E. Petty, *Journal of Personality and Social Psychology,* 1982, vol. 42, pp. 116–131). All you need to say is:

> Subjects were presented with Cacioppo and Petty's (1982) Need for Cognition Scale. This is an 18-item measure of the tendency to engage in and enjoy thinking.

Incidentally, if your research project is in some area of social psychology or personality, two valuable reference books are Marvin E. Shaw and Jack M. Wright's *Scales for the Measurement of Attitudes* (McGraw-Hill) and John P. Robinson, Phillip R. Shaver, and Lawrence S. Wrightsman's *Measures of Personality and Social Psychological Attitudes* (Academic Press). These books may save you from having to "reinvent the wheel" because they contain a number of actual scales, facts on reliability and validity, and details on how to administer and score the scales.

# Results

In the next major section, describe your findings. You might plan to show the results in a table, as in Tables 1 and 2 of John's report. Do not make your instructor guess what you were thinking; label your table fully, and discuss the data in the narrative of this section so that it is clear what the numbers represent. It is not necessary to repeat the results from the table in your narrative; simply tell what they mean.

The results section should consist of a careful, detailed analysis that strikes a balance between being discursive and being falsely or needlessly precise:

> ➤ You are guilty of **false precision** when something inherently vague is presented in overly precise terms. Suppose you used one of the attitude scales in Shaw and Wright's book in your research, and suppose the research participants indicated their attitudinal responses by using a 5-point scale of "strongly agree" to "strongly disagree." It would be falsely precise to report the means to a high number of decimal places, because your scale was not that sensitive to slight variations in attitudes.
>
> ➤ You are guilty of **needless precision** when (almost without thinking about it) you report something much more exactly than the circumstances require. For

example, reporting the weight of mouse subjects to six decimal places might be within the bounds of your measuring instrument, but the situation does not call for such exactitude.

Note on page 10 of John's report that he states that the $p$ value of one of his results is .00000001. Is this a case of needless precision? Most researchers simply give a ballpark estimate of $p$; for example, they might report that $p < .05$. Another approach is to report a precise $p$ value; the convention is to report two digits after the initial 0's (for example, .064, .0071, .00011, .000092). However, for many purposes a single such digit after the initial 0's will suffice. Of course, if you are looking up $p$ values in a statistical table (that is, instead of using a computer program or a scientific calculator), you may not have the option of reporting them precisely. Thus, it also is conventional to state only that $p$ was less than (" $<$ ") or greater than (" $>$ ") some particular column value in the statistical table.

Incidentally, knowing the exact $p$ can be a valuable piece of information if a reader wanted to use your data as part of a **meta-analysis** (that is, an analysis of a set of studies). Instead of ending a research report with the usual clarion call for further research, a meta-analysis summarizes the available studies in terms of significance levels or effect sizes. If you are interested in knowing more about meta-analysis, you might begin with Richard J. Light and David B. Pillemer's *Summing Up: The Science of Reviewing Research* (Harvard University Press). If you would like a user-friendly introduction to the basics of summarizing $p$ values and effect sizes, consult Appendix C in *Beginning Behavioral Research: A Conceptual Primer*, by Ralph L. Rosnow and Robert Rosenthal (Macmillan). If you are interested in a comprehensive discussion of all aspects of meta-analysis, see *The Handbook of Research Synthesis*, edited by Harris Cooper and Larry V. Hedges (Russell Sage Foundation, 1994).

Ask yourself the following questions as you structure your results section:

➤ What did I find?
➤ How can I say what I found in a careful, detailed way?
➤ Is what I am planning to say precise and to the point?
➤ Am I being overly or misleadingly exact?

➤ Will what I have said be clear to the reader?
➤ Have I left out anything of importance?

# Discussion

In the discussion section you will use the facts you have gathered to form a cohesive unit. A review of the introductory section is often helpful. Think about how you will discuss your research findings in light of your original hypothesis. Did **serendipity** play a role in your study? The term comes from Serendip, once the name for Sri Lanka; it was claimed that the three princes of Serendip were always making discoveries by good luck. If serendipity has played a role in your study, detail the unexpected by-products and ideas.

Try to write "defensively" without being too blatant about it. That is, be your own devil's advocate and ask yourself what a skeptical reader might see as the other side of your argument or conclusion. In particular, look for shortcomings or critical inconsistencies, and anticipate the reader's reaction to them. If you cannot find any holes in your argument or conclusion, ask a clever friend to help you out.

Here are some additional questions to consider as you begin to structure this section:

➤ What was the purpose of my study?
➤ How do my results relate to that purpose?
➤ Did I make any serendipitous findings of interest?
➤ How valid and generalizable are my findings?
➤ Are there larger implications in these findings?
➤ Is there an alternative way to interpret my results?

You might wish to plan a separate conclusions section if you feel more comfortable with that format or have a lot to cover that you would like to separate from the main body of your discussion. However, it is quite proper to treat the final paragraph or two of your discussion section as the conclusion. In either case, your conclusions should be stated as clearly and concisely as possible.

If there were larger implications, this would be the place to spell them out. Are there implications for further research? If so, suggest them here. John raises the external validity issue in the final paragraph of his discussion, in which he talks about the need to replicate his findings in other naturalistic settings.

# References

Once you have made plans for writing the body of the report, give some thought to your reference material again. You will need to include an alphabetized listing of all the sources of information from which you drew. To avoid retracing your steps in the library, keep **a running list** of the material that will appear in this section as you progress through the early preparation of the report. If you are using a word processor, add each reference to the back of the report as you cite it in your narrative. If you are using the index-card method, make a separate card for each reference that you actually use in your report; it will be a simple matter later to alphabetize the cards and make sure that none have been omitted.

# Appendix

The purpose of this final section is to display the raw materials and computations of your investigation. For example, if you used a lengthy questionnaire or test (which cannot be adequately presented in the limited space of the method section), then include it in the appendix. John's questionnaire was so brief and straightforward that he was able to present it fully in a couple of sentences, but he includes his statistical calculations in the appendix.

Your instructor may not require an appendix or may stipulate a different list of items to be included. Keep all of your notes and data until the instructor returns your report and you receive a grade in the course, just in case your instructor has questions about your work.

# Organizing Your Thoughts

In the preceding chapter we described how to make an outline for the term paper; the research report does not require a gross outline because its formal structure already provides a skeleton waiting to be fleshed out. Nevertheless, all researchers find it absolutely essential to organize their thoughts about each section before writing the first draft. There are three ways to do this:

> ➤ If you like to work with a detailed sentence outline, then examine Chapter 3 for guidelines.

➤ You can make notes on separate index cards for each major point (for example, the rationale of the study, the derivation of each hypothesis, and each background study) and draw on these notes to write your first draft.

➤ If you are using a word processor, you can simply make a file of such notes.

If you are still having a hard time getting going, here are two more tips:

➤ Imagine you are sitting across a table from a friend; tell your "friend" what you found.

➤ Take a pocket tape recorder for a walk; tell it what you found in your research.

No matter what approach you favor, make sure that your notes or files are accurate and complete. If you are summarizing someone else's study, then you must note the full citation. If you are quoting someone, include the statement in quotation marks and make sure that you have copied it exactly.

# CHAPTER FIVE

# Writing and Revising

*Writing a first draft is a little like taking the first dip in chilly ocean waters on a hot day. It may be uncomfortable at the outset but feels better once you get used to it. In this chapter we provide some pointers to buoy you up as you begin writing. We shall also provide tips to help you revise your work.*

## Focusing on the Objective

At this stage of your work, you should have an ordered set of notes and an outline, in the case of the term paper, or a given structure if your project is a research report. The material you have assembled can be thought of as the bare bones of the paper. Sentences and paragraphs will be combined now to fill out the skeleton.

To begin the first draft, write down somewhere the purpose or goal you have in mind (that is, what your paper will be about). Make this **self-motivator statement** succinct so that you have a focus for your thoughts as you begin to set them down on paper or enter them into a word processor.

If we refer to the two sample papers, we can imagine the following self-motivators:

### From Maria

I'm going to write an expository paper that will describe two general modes of treatment for anorexia nervosa.

## From John

> My research report will focus on whether people are more likely
> to pass on rumors they believe are true than rumors they believe
> are false.

This trick of using a self-motivator statement can help to concentrate your thoughts and make the task of writing seem less formidable. The self-motivator is a good way simply to get you going and keep you clear-headed. You will be less apt to go off on a tangent if you remind yourself exactly where you want your paper to go.

# The Opening

A good opening is crucial if you want to engage the reader's attention and interest. Some psychologists are masters at writing good openings, but most articles and books in this and related fields (as you discovered in your literature search) start out ponderously. There are enough cases of ponderous writing that we do not need to give examples. But what about openings that grip our minds and make us want to delve further into the work?

One way to begin your paper in an inviting way is to pose a stimulating question. For example, Sissela Bok opened her book *Lying: Moral Choice in Public and Private Life* (Pantheon, 1978) with a number of questions:

> Should physicians lie to dying patients so as to delay the fear and
> anxiety which the truth might bring them? Should professors exaggerate the excellence of their students on recommendations in
> order to give them a better chance in a tight job market? Should
> parents conceal from children the fact that they were adopted?
> Should social scientists send investigators masquerading as patients to physicians in order to learn about racial and sexual biases
> in diagnosis and treatment? Should government lawyers lie to
> Congressmen who might otherwise oppose a much-needed
> welfare bill? And should journalists lie to those from whom they
> seek information in order to expose corruption? (p. xv)

Does this opening make you want to read further? Another technique is to impress on readers the paradoxical nature of a timely issue. Stanley Milgram, in *Obedience to Authority* (Harper, 1969), began as follows:

Obedience is as basic an element in the structure of social life as one can point to. Some system of authority is a requirement of all communal living, and it is only the man dwelling in isolation who is not forced to respond, through defiance or submission, to the commands of others. Obedience, as a determinant of behavior, is of particular relevance to our time. It has been reliably established that from 1933 to 1945 millions of innocent people were systematically slaughtered on command. Gas chambers were built, death camps were guarded, daily quotas of corpses were produced with the same efficiency as the manufacture of appliances. These inhumane policies may have originated in the mind of a single person, but they could only have been carried out on a massive scale if a very large number of people obeyed orders.[1] (p. 1)

However, perhaps you are thinking, "What does Milgram's or Bok's work have to do with me? These are Ph.D. psychologists who were writing for publication, and I'm just writing a paper for a course." The answer any instructor will give you is that an expectation of good writing is not limited to published work (for example, it is expected in business correspondence, company memos, and applications for jobs). Anne A. Skleder, whose 1993 Ph.D. research was on interpersonal intelligence, opened her unpublished dissertation with the following passage:

We speak of intelligence every day, in many different contexts. Some individuals are referred to as "book smart," strong in verbal or mathematical skills which are closely linked with common conceptions of intelligence. Others are considered to be "street-wise" or "street-smart," astute in the ways of the world.

What makes Skleder's opening paragraph inviting? It strikes a resonant chord in the reader. There are many other useful opening techniques: a definition, an anecdote, a metaphor that compares or contrasts, an epigraph (an opening quotation), and so on—all of these are devices that a writer can use to shape a beginning paragraph. Not only should it draw the reader into the work, but it should also serve to provide momentum for the writer as his or her words and ideas begin to flow. Maria begins her paper by pointing up a paradox, while John borrows lines from a classic poem to underscore the long history of his topic.

---

[1]This passage was written before there were concerns about sexist language, but Milgram's use of the word *man* ("it is only the man dwelling in isolation") as a generic term for men and women is now considered improper usage. Instead, he could have said "people dwelling in isolation"; we return to this issue later.

# Settling Down to Write

Should you find yourself still having trouble beginning the introductory paragraph, try the trick of not starting at the opening of your paper. Start writing whatever section you feel will be the easiest, and then tackle the rest as your ideas begin to flow. When faced with the blank page or blank computer screen and flashing cursor, some students escape by taking a nap or watching MTV. Recognize these counterproductive moves for what they are, and use them instead as rewards after you have done your work.

The following are general pointers to ensure that your writing will go as smoothly as possible:

➤ While writing, try to work in a quiet, well-lighted place in two-hour stretches.

➤ Go for a walk by yourself to collect your thoughts and to think of a sentence to get you going again.

➤ If you are typing your first draft, double- or triple-space it so you will have room for legible revisions. If you are writing on a notepad, skip a line for each line you write down. If you are using a word processor, modify the system format to double-space your printout.

➤ Be sure to number the pages you write. If you are using a word processor, modify the system format so the page numbers will automatically appear as shown in Maria's and John's papers.

➤ When you take a break, try to stop at a point that is midway through an idea or a paragraph. In this way you can resume work where you left off and avoid feeling stuck or having to start cold. If you are using a word processor, type in a line of XXX's to show yourself where you left off.

➤ Try to pace your work with time to spare so that you can complete the first draft and let it rest for 24 hours. When you return to the completed first draft after a break, your critical powers will be enhanced, and you will have a fresh approach to shaping the final draft.

# Ethics of Writing and Reporting

In 1992, the American Psychological Association (APA) revised its ethical principles for professional psychologists (see *American*

*Psychologist,* December 1992) to include guidelines for authors. Some of these standards also have implications for students who are writing papers, for example:

> ➤ One guideline in the new APA code is that psychologists are responsible for making available the data on which their conclusions are based. The implication for students writing research reports is that they also are generally expected to produce all of their raw data as required by the instructor.

> ➤ Second, it is unethical to misrepresent original research by publishing it in more than one journal and implying that each report represents a different study. The implication for students is that it is also unethical to submit the same work for additional credit in different courses.

> ➤ Third, psychologist authors are expected to give credit where it is due. The implication for a student is that if someone gave you an idea, you should credit that person in a footnote.

However, the most fundamental ethical principle is honesty and accuracy. Scientists and scholars in all disciplines abhor dishonesty and sloppiness, and they expect their students to uphold the same standards. Being honest and accurate also means never plagiarizing, even accidentally.

## Avoiding Plagiarism

The term **plagiarism,** which comes from a Latin word meaning "kidnapper," refers to stealing another person's ideas or work and passing them off as your own. A recent book on this subject is Thomas Mallon's *Stolen Words: Forays into the Origins and Ravages of Plagiarism* (Penguin). In one fascinating case described by Mallon, CBS television and the creators of *Falcon Crest* were sued for plagiarism by the author of a novel about the California wine country. It is crucial that you understand what constitutes plagiarism and its consequences for those who commit it. Plagiarism in student writing is often accidental, but it is important to avoid "kidnapping" someone else's work even unintentionally. For students, the penalties for plagiarism in a class assignment can be severe.

This warning does not mean that you cannot use other people's ideas or work in your writing. What it does mean is that you must give the author of that material full credit for originality and must not misrepresent (intentionally or accidentally) that material as your own original work. To illustrate, suppose a student submitted a term paper containing the following passage:

> Deceit and violence are two forms of deliberate assault on human beings. Both can coerce people into acting against their will. Most harm that can happen to people through violence can also happen to them through deceit. However, deceit controls more subtly, because it works on belief as well as action. Even Othello, whom few would have dared to try to subdue by force, could be brought to destroy himself and Desdemona through falsehood.

Sounds like an "A" paper? Yes, but the student would receive an "F." The reason for the student's failure is plagiarism. The student stole the passage out of Sissela Bok's work. In *Lying: Moral Choice in Public and Private Life*, Bok states:

> Deceit and violence—these are the two forms of deliberate assault on human beings. Both can coerce people into acting against their will. Most harm that can befall victims through violence can come to them also through deceit. But deceit controls more subtly, for it works on belief as well as action. Even Othello, whom few would have dared to try to subdue by force, could be brought to destroy himself and Desdemona through falsehood. (p. 18)

How might the student have used Bok's work without falling into plagiarism? The answer is simply to put quotes around the material you want to copy verbatim—and then give a complete citation. Even if you want simply to paraphrase the work, you are still responsible for giving full credit to the original author. A reasonable paraphrase might appear as follows:

> Bok (1978) makes the case that both deceit and violence "can coerce people into acting against their will" (p. 18). Deceit, she notes, controls more subtly, because it affects belief. Using a literary analogy, she observes: "Even Othello, whom few would have dared to try to subdue by force, could be brought to destroy himself and Desdemona through falsehood" (p. 18).

## Lazy Writing

Some lazy students, upon hearing that quotations and citations are not construed by definition as plagiarism, submit papers saturated with quoted material. Unless you feel it absolutely essential, avoid quoting long passages throughout a paper. It will be necessary to quote or paraphrase some material (with a citation, of course), but your written work is expected to result from your own individual effort. Quoting a simple sentence that can easily be paraphrased signals lazy writing.

In other words, your paper should reflect *your* thoughts on a particular topic after you have carefully examined and synthesized material from the sources you feel are pertinent. The penalty for lazy writing is not as severe as that for plagiarism, although it often is still a reduced grade. Avoid both problems: plagiarism and lazy writing. As noted earlier, it is a good idea to keep your note cards, outlines, and rough drafts, because some instructors will ask students for such material if a question arises about the originality of their work.

And finally, many students use terms that they do not understand, especially when dealing with technical material—anatomical or statistical terms, for example. Although this usage is not considered plagiarism, it does constitute lazy writing (and bad scholarship as well). Always try to make your point in your own words. If someone else has said it much better than you ever can hope to say it, quote (and cite) or paraphrase (and cite) the other source. On the other hand, if you really cannot say it in your own words, then you do not understand it well enough to write about it.

## Tone

As you write, there are certain basic style points to keep in mind. The **tone** of your paper refers to the manner in which you express your ideas to the reader. Your writing should not be dull; presumably you are writing on a topic that you find fascinating, inasmuch as you chose it.

Here are some hints on how to create the right tone:

➤ Strive for an explicit, straightforward, interesting, but not emotional, way of expressing your thoughts, findings, and conclusions.

➤ Avoid having your term paper or research report read like a letter to a favorite aunt ("Here's what Jones and Smith say . . ." or "So I told the research participants . . .").

➤ Do not try to duplicate a journalist's slick style, familiar in the glib spoken reports on network TV and in super- market tabloids.

➤ It is all right to use the first person ("I shall discuss . . ." or "My conclusion is that . . ."). However, do not refer to yourself as *we*, unless you have a multiple per- sonality and all of you collaborated on the paper ("We observed that . . ." or "In this paper we will explore . . .").

➤ Strive for an objective, direct tone that keeps your reader subordinate to the material you are presenting. Do not write, "The reader will note that the results were . . ." Instead, write, "The results were . . ."

➤ A famous writing manual is that by William Strunk Jr. and E. B. White, *The Elements of Style* (Macmillan). One of Professor Strunk's admonitions is "Omit needless words. Omit needless words. Omit needless words."

Examine the following excerpts taken from the sample papers to see how the tone used by the student can color the impact of the paper. John states his hypothesis in response to a question he poses that piques our interest; he uses the impersonal pronoun *one* to make a general statement and in this way avoids the awkward *he/she* or *s/he* contraction that inexperienced writers may use:

## From John's Research Report

Why is it that some rumors are transmitted with greater alacrity than others during stressful situations? In this study it was hypothesized that the more confidence one has in the truth of a rumor, the more likely one is to transmit the rumor.

Maria also describes the problem she chose to study in a tone that is compelling but not melodramatic or slick, and she uses the first person *I* to draw the reader into her paper:

## From Maria's Term Paper

There are, of course, several other recognizable types of eating disorders (American Psychiatric Association, 1987), but in this term paper I will concentrate on what I perceive as two general orien- tations in the treatment of anorexia nervosa.

# Nonsexist Language

The question of **word gender** has recently become a matter of some sensitivity among many writers, particularly in psychology and related areas. One reason to discourage sex bias in written and spoken communication is that words can influence people's thoughts and deeds, and we do not want to reinforce stereotypes or prejudiced behavior. To be sure, there is sometimes a good reason not to use gender-free pronouns. Suppose a new drug has been tested only on male subjects. If the researchers used only gender-free pronouns when referring to their participants, a reader might mistakenly infer that the results apply to both sexes.

The point, of course, is to think before you write. In her book *The Elements of Nonsexist Usage* (Prentice-Hall, 1990), Val Dumond made the following observation concerning overuse of the word *man*: "When the word is used, that is the mental picture that is formed. The picture is what simultaneously represents a conceptual meaning to the interpreter. Since a female picture does not come to mind when the word *man* is used, it would follow that *man* does not represent in any way a female human" (p. 1).

When the issues of sexist language first gained prominence in psychology, researchers and others often used contrived terms such as *s/he* and *he/she* to avoid sexist language. Experienced writers and editors have proposed various ways to circumvent the awkwardness of such contractions and also the possible trap of gender-free language. In general, beware of masculine nouns and pronouns that can give a sex bias to your writing. There are two simple rules:

> ➤ Use plural pronouns when you are referring to both genders, for instance, "They did . . ." instead of "He did . . ." or ". . . to them" instead of ". . . to him."
> ➤ Use masculine and feminine pronouns if the situation calls for them. For example, if the study you are discussing used only male research participants, then the masculine pronouns are accurate; the contraction *he/she* or *s/he* would mislead the reader into thinking that the research participants were both women and men.

# Voice

The verb forms you use in your writing can speak with one of two voices: active or passive. You write in the **active voice** when you represent the subject of your sentence as performing the action expressed by your verb ("The research participants responded by . . ."). You write in the **passive voice** when the subject of your sentence undergoes the action expressed by your verb ("The response made by the research participants was . . .").

If you try to rely mainly on the active voice, then you will have a more vital, compelling style:

### Active Voice (Good)

Dollard and Miller hypothesized that frustration leads to aggression.

### Passive Voice (Not as Good)

It was hypothesized by Dollard and Miller that frustration leads to aggression.

However, the passive voice sometimes is useful in avoiding the gender traps of singular masculine pronouns when you actually mean to refer to both sexes. For example:

### Active (Gender Trap)

If the subject reacted in this way, it was taken to be a clear indication of his political attitude.

### Passive (No Gender Trap)

A particular political attitude was clearly indicated by the subject's reaction.

# Verb Tense

The verb tense you use in your paper can get into a tangle unless you observe the following basic rules:

> ▶ Use the **past tense** to report studies that were done in the past ("Jones and Smith found . . ."). If you are

writing a research report, then both method and results sections call for the past tense because your study has already been accomplished ("In this study, rumors *were* collected . . ." and "In these 55 questionnaires there *were* . . .").

➤ Use the **present tense** to define terms ("Anorexia nervosa, in clinical parlance, *refers* to . . ." and "Rumor *is* traditionally defined as . . ."). The present tense is also frequently used to state a general hypothesis or to make a general claim ("A current rumor theory *suggests* that the strength of a rumor *is* determined by . . .").

➤ The **future tense** can be saved for the section of your paper in which you discuss implications for further investigation ("Future research *will be* necessary . . ."), but it is not essential to use the future tense. For instance, John uses the present tense effectively ("Further investigation *is* warranted . . .").

## Agreement of Subject and Verb

Make sure each sentence expresses a complete thought and has a **subject** (in general terms, something that performs the action) and a **verb** (an action that is performed or a state of being).

### Subject and Verb Agree

Participants [**subject**] were [**verb**] faculty members.

Because the subject is plural (*participants*), the verb form used (*were*) is also plural. This means the verb and subject agree, a basic rule of grammar.

In most sentence forms, achieving this agreement is a simple matter. But trouble can sometimes arise, so here are some tips:

➤ When you use **collective nouns** (those that name a group), they can be either singular or plural, for example, *committee, team, faculty.* When you think of the group as a single unit, use a singular verb ("The administration *is* ready to settle"). Plurals are called for when you want to refer to the components of a group ("The faculty *were* divided on the strike issue").

➤ Trouble can pop up when words come between subject and verb: "Therapy [**singular subject**], in combination with behavioral organic methods of weight gain, exemplifies [**singular verb form**] this approach." It would be incorrect to write: "Therapy, in combination with behavioral organic methods of weight gain, *exemplify* [**plural verb form**] this approach.

➤ Use a **singular verb form** after the following: *each, either, everyone, someone, neither, nobody.* Here is a correct usage: "When everyone is ready, the experiment will begin."

## Common Usage Errors

Instructors see frequent usage errors in student papers. The inside front cover of this manual lists pairs of words that are both pronounced similarly (**homonyms**) and often confused with one another, such as *accept* ("receive") and *except* ("other than").

Another pair of confusing homonyms is *affect* and *effect*. In their most common form, the words *effect*, a noun meaning "outcome" (as in "aggression is often an *effect* of frustration"), and *affect*, a verb meaning "to influence" (as in "frustration can *affect* how a person behaves"), are frequently confused. Moreover, *effect* can also be a verb meaning "to bring about" (as in "the procedure *effected* a measurable improvement"), and, in psychology, *affect* can be a noun meaning *emotion* (as in "subjects may show a positive *affect*").

Another potential source of problems is the incorrect use of the singular and plural of some familiar terms, for instance:

| *Singular* | *Plural* |
|---|---|
| analysis | analyses |
| anomaly | anomalies |
| appendix | appendixes or appendices (both are correct) |
| criterion | criteria |
| datum | data |
| hypothesis | hypotheses |
| phenomenon | phenomena |
| stimulus | stimuli |

For example, one common usage error is the confusion of *phenomena* [**plural term**] with *phenomenon* [**singular term**]. It would be incorrect to write "This [**singular pronoun**] phenomena [**plural** subject] is [**singular verb**] of interest." The correct form is either "This phenomenon is . . ." or "These phenomena are . . ."

Another common error results from the confusion of *data* [**plural term**] with *datum* [**singular term**]. It would be incorrect to write "The data [**plural subject**] indicates [**singular verb**] . . ." The correct form is "The data indicate . . ."

One common source of confusion is in the misuse of the words *between* and *among*. As a general rule, use *between* when you are referring to two items only; use *among* when there are more than two items. If you accept this, it would be incorrect to write "between the three of them."

There is, however, one anachronism that you can do nothing about correcting. In the analysis of variance (called *ANOVA*), conventional usage says, "between sum of squares" and the "between-mean square," even if the number of conditions being compared is more than two.

Other common problems concern the use of some *prefixes* in psychological terms:

➤ The prefix *inter-* means "between" (for example, *interpersonal* means "between persons"); the prefix *intra-* means "within" (for example, *intrapersonal* means "within the person").

➤ The prefix *intro-* means "inward" or "within"; the prefix *extra-* means "outside" or "beyond." The psychological term *introverted* thus refers to an "inner-directed personality"; the term *extraverted* indicates an "outer-directed personality."

➤ The prefix *hyper-* means "too much"; the prefix *hypo-* means "too little." Hence, the term *hypothyroidism* refers to a deficiency of thyroid hormone, while *hyperthyroidism* denotes an excess of thyroid hormone and a *hyperactive* child is one who is excessively active.

## Punctuation

Correct use of the various punctuation marks will help avoid confusion in your writing. A **period** ends a declarative sentence. It also follows an abbreviation, as in the following common abbreviations of Latin words:

| | |
|---|---|
| cf. | from *confer* ("compare") |
| e.g. | from *exempli gratia* ("for example") |
| et al. | from *et alia* ("and others") |
| et seq. | from *et sequens* ("and following") |
| ibid. | from *ibidem* ("in the same place") |
| i.e. | from *id est* ("that is") |
| op. cit. | from *opere citato* ("in the work cited") |
| viz. | from *videlicet* ("namely") |

If you continually write *eg.* or *et. al.* in your paper, you will be waving a red flag, telling the instructor, "I don't know the meaning of these terms!" The reason, of course, is that *e.g.* is the abbreviation for two words, not one; *eg.* announces that you believe it is the abbreviation of one word. Putting a period after *et* tells the instructor that you believe it is an abbreviation, which it is not.

On the subject of abbreviations, some others that you may encounter in the library are the short forms of English words:

| | |
|---|---|
| anon. | for *anonymous* |
| ch. | for *chapter* |
| diagr. | for *diagram* |
| ed. | for *editor* or *edition* |
| fig. | for *figure* |
| ms. | for *manuscript* |
| p. | for *page* |
| pp. | for *pages* |
| rev. | for *revised* |
| vol. | for *volume* |

The various uses of the *comma* include the following:

➤ Use commas to separate three or more items in a series ("Smith, Jones, and Brown" or "high, medium, and low scorers").

➤ Use commas to set off introductory phrases in a sentence ("In another experiment performed 10 years later, the same researchers found . . .").

➤ Use commas to set off thoughts or phrases that are incidental to or that qualify the basic idea of the sentence ("This variable, although not part of the researchers' central hypothesis, was also examined").

➤ Put a comma before connecting words (*and, but, or, nor, yet*) when they join independent clauses ("The subject lost weight, but he was still able to . . .").

The **semicolon** (;) is used to join independent clauses in a sentence when connecting words are omitted. A semicolon is called for when the thoughts in the two independent clauses are close, and the writer wishes to emphasize this point or to contrast the two thoughts:

### Semicolon for Connecting Thoughts

Anorexia nervosa is a disorder in which the victims literally starve themselves; despite their emaciated appearance, they consider themselves overweight.

In most instances these long sentences can be divided into shorter ones, which will be clearer:

### No Semicolon

Anorexia nervosa is a disorder in which the victims literally starve themselves. Despite their emaciated appearance, they consider themselves overweight.

Use a **colon** (:) to indicate that a list will follow, to introduce a quotation, or to introduce an amplification. The colon tells the reader, "Note what follows":

### Colon to Indicate That a List Follows

Subjects were given the following items: (1) four calling birds, (2) three French hens, (3) two turtle doves . . .

### Colon to Indicate That a Quote Follows

Subject B responded: "My feeling about this ridiculous situation is that we should leave."

### Colon to Introduce an Amplification (for example, John's subtitle)

Confidence in Rumor and the Likelihood of Transmission: A Correlational Study

# Quotations

**Double quotation marks** (" ") are used to enclose direct quotations in the narrative of the paper, and **single quotation marks** (' ') indicate a quote within a quote:

## Quotation Marks

Subject B responded: "My feeling about this difficult situation was summed up in a nutshell by Jim when he said, 'It's a tough job, but somebody has got to do it.'"

Here are more rules about punctuation when you are using quotations in your paper:

➤ If the appropriate punctuation is a comma or a period, it is included *within* the quotation marks.
➤ Colons and semicolons always come *after* the closing quotation marks.
➤ When the quotation is more than four typed or handwritten lines, it is set off from the body of the prose by means of indented margins, and quotation marks are omitted.

## Passage Containing Lengthy Quotation and Internal Quotation

What practical implications do Rosenthal and Jacobson (1968) draw from their research findings? They write:

> As teacher-training institutions begin to teach the possibility that teachers' expectations of their pupils' performance may serve as self-fulfilling prophecies, there may be a new expectancy created. The new expectancy may be that children can learn more than had been believed possible, an expectation held by many educational theorists, though for quite different reasons. . . . The new expectancy, at the very least, will make it more difficult when they encounter the educationally disadvantaged for teachers to think, "Well, after all, what can you expect?" The man on the street may be permitted his opinions and prophecies of the unkempt children loitering in a dreary schoolyard. The teacher in the schoolroom may need to learn that those same prophecies within her may be fulfilled; she is no casual passer-by. Perhaps Pygmalion in the classroom is more her role. (pp. 181–182)

Notice that the quotation begins, "As teacher-training institutions . . ." and ends ". . . in the classroom is more her role"; the page numbers on which this passage appears in Rosenthal and Jacobson's book are shown in parentheses at the end.

This passage (like that by Milgram, quoted previously) was written before there were concerns about the question of assigning gender, and the authors refer to "the man on the street" and to the teacher as "she." If you wished to make the point that the quoted passage ignores gender, then you might insert in brackets the word *sic* (Latin, meaning "thus," denoting that a word or phrase that appears strange or incorrect has been quoted verbatim). The two sentences would then look like this:

> The man [sic] on the street may be permitted his opinions and prophecies of the unkempt children loitering in a dreary schoolyard. The teacher in the schoolroom may need to learn that those same prophecies within her [sic] may be fulfilled; she is no casual passer-by.

Note that we did not insert *sic* after every gender term in the quoted passage. In the first sentence, the masculine pronoun *his* is not set off by *sic* inasmuch as the referent is "man on the street." In the second sentence, the feminine pronoun *she* is also not set off, because the referent is "within her."

# Revising

In the next chapter we consider the details of assembling and producing your final draft. Whether you are using a word processor or a typewriter, **revising** the first draft of your paper is best done after you have been able to leave the material entirely. When you approach your writing after having taken such a break (ideally, 24 hours or more), your critical powers will be sharper. Syntax errors, lapses in logic, and other problems will become evident, so that smoothing out these sections will be a relatively simple chore.

As you reread, consider the following "dos" and "don'ts":

➤ Be concise.
➤ Break up long paragraphs that contain a lot of disparate ideas into smaller, more coherent paragraphs.
➤ Be specific.
➤ Choose words for what they mean, not just for how they sound.
➤ Double-check punctuation.

➤ Don't use a long word when a short one will do.
➤ Don't be redundant ("most unique").
➤ Don't let spelling errors mar your writing.

If you are revising your first draft in longhand or with a typewriter, equip yourself with scissors and glue (retractable stick glue is the easiest to use). With these tools, rearranging paragraphs, condensing sentences, and adding or subtracting references will be less painful. The least painful recourse, however, is to use a word processor.

## Using a Word Processor

If you are working with a *word processor* (that is, a personal computer that uses a word-processing program), then you know that the steps involved in first drafts, revisions, and final drafts are telescoped. These stages lose their formal definition because the computer allows you, with the stroke of a key, to shift or change words, sentences, paragraphs, even entire sections as you compose. Notes, long quotations, references, tables, and even figures can be stored in the computer's memory or on a disk and retrieved as needed. A word processor releases the writer from an enormous amount of drudgery, even though it cannot substitute for the hard work of organizing ideas, thinking them through, and expressing them clearly.

Many word-processing programs also contain a dictionary (actually, a word inventory) that allows you to monitor your spelling of common English words. It can be very useful, but it can also lull students into a false sense of security. Many terms that psychologists and other professionals use may not appear in your word-processing inventory. A simple way to deal with this problem is to add words as you come across unusual terms. Start by adding the terms that appear inside the front and back covers of this manual. Other relevant terms will become evident as you go about your literature search; keep a list, and then enter these terms into your system when you have a free moment.

If you are new to word processing (or are learning a new word-processing program), be sure you know how to save and back up your work when you are ready to start composing. Some systems do this for you automatically at regular intervals, but it is a good idea to do it at least every hour or so. You never known when the electricity will suddenly go out or someone will playfully or accidentally hit the erase key, sending your work into oblivion. Making a "backup" means not only storing something inside the computer's hard drive (that is, if it's *your* PC) but also copying it onto a disk. Our habit is also to make a printout (called a *hard copy*) at the end of the day. Having a printed copy will allow you to inspect and modify the final layout to make sure it looks the way you want it to. It also allows you to polish your writing in a format that is tangible. Sometimes spelling errors and murky passages that are less apparent on-screen jump out as your eye traverses a printed page.

Finally, do not expect a perfect result on the first draft or even the second draft. Putting thoughts down and then revising them is a way of showing yourself that you have made progress. It gives you something concrete to work on as you proceed to the final draft.

# CHAPTER SIX

# Layout and Production

*Whether you are using a word processor or a typewriter, you need to be concerned about the layout of your research report or term paper. This chapter, which uses Maria's and John's papers as illustrative models, provides you with tips and general guidelines for developing a finished product.*

## The First Impression

Study the sample passage at the top of Exhibit 11. If you were the instructor and a student submitted a paper to you that began with this paragraph, what would your first impression be? How many problems do you count?

- Corrected typographical error: Pygmaliom
- Spelling mistake: Jacobsen (twice)
- Usage error: phenomena
- Corrected omission: statistically significant
- Spelling mistake: surpased
- Usage error: &
- Typographical error: inthe
- Spelling mistake: intellectule

With a little time and effort the paragraph could have been cleaned up to enhance the student's finished product. Compare the messy paragraph with the carefully edited and cleanly prepared version below it to see what a difference a first impression can make.

**EXHIBIT 11**  First impressions count!

In Pygmaliom in the Classroom, Rosenthal and Jacobsen (1968) conclude that the phenomena of the self-fulfilling prophecy is as viable in the classroom as Rosenthal and his coworkers previously showed it to be in the scientist's laboratory.  Students whose names were randomly selected and who were represented to be "bloomers" showed IQ gains that surpased those of students not so labeled for their teachers.  It was the label, Rosenthal & Jacobsen assert, which created false positive expectations inthe teachers' minds and, in turn, resulted in this difference in intellectule performance.

In Pygmalion in the Classroom, Rosenthal and Jacobsen (1968) conclude that the phenomenon of the self-fulfilling prophecy is as viable in the classroom as Rosenthal and his coworkers previously showed it to be in the scientist's laboratory.  Students whose names were randomly selected and who were represented to be "bloomers" showed statistically significant IQ gains that surpassed those of students not so labeled for their teachers.  It was the label, Rosenthal and Jacobson assert, which created false positive expectations in the teachers' minds and, in turn, resulted in this difference in intellectual performance.

In the previous chapter we advised you to make backup copies if you were working with a word processor. Another reason for having a backup hard copy (that is, a printout) is that it allows you to evaluate and polish the layout of the anticipated finished product. However, the hard copy may look deceptively clean, so do not be captivated by the finished look of the printed page. Check it carefully against the sample papers for layout, and also make sure it is not flawed by errors of omission or lapses in logic.

# General Pointers

We assume (as your instructor does) that you will correct spelling mistakes, usage errors, and omissions before you submit your paper.

What follows are general pointers as you set about typing or processing that final draft:

➤ If you are typing the paper, treat yourself to a new typewriter ribbon. If you are using a word processor, find out if there is a laser printer you can use. If you are using an impact printer, make sure it has a fresh ribbon. It will be frustrating for the instructor to have to read a paper with script so light or blurry that it taxes the eyes.

➤ If you are typing the paper, use 8½ × 11-inch white paper, preferably bond. Never use onionskin paper; it tears easily and does not take corrections well. Do not use commercial "erasable" paper; it smears readily.

➤ Use double line spacing, and print or type on only one side of the paper, numbering the pages in the upper-right corner as the sample papers illustrate.

➤ Make an extra copy of the finished paper, whether you are typing it or using a word processor. The original is for your instructor, and the duplicate copy will ensure the availability of an exact spare copy in case of an unforeseen problem.

➤ If you are using a word processor and do not have access to a laser, ink-jet, or daisy-wheel printer, use the strikeover (or letter-quality) mode rather than the first-draft mode to print your final copy.

➤ If you are using a word processor, let the right margin remain ragged (uneven). That is, do not use a justified right margin: it creates a block effect and sometimes odd spacing within lines. It is better to stick with a ragged right margin.

➤ Use generous margins to leave space for the instructor to make comments. When typing, set your pica typewriter at 55 characters per line; on an elite typewriter, use 66 characters per line.

We turn now to other specifics of layout and processing (or typing) that will help to give your finished product an inviting appearance.

## Title Page Format

Glance at the title pages of Maria's and John's papers. Note that the title of the term paper or research report summarizes the main idea of the project and is centered on the page. A good title is succinct; yet, at a glance, it adequately describes to the reader the gist of the work. You will already have arrived at a working title when you narrowed your topic. That title can now be changed or made more specific if you feel it is no longer accurate or completely descriptive of the finished project.

Other information is also shown on the title page of Maria's and John's papers:

- The student's name
- The course or sequence for which the paper was written
- The date the paper was turned in

It is optional to show the instructor's name (if the paper is submitted for a course) or the adviser's name (if the paper is submitted to fulfill some other requirement). However, if the paper is a senior honors thesis, you should include an acknowledgment page (after the title page) on which you thank your adviser and any others who extended a helping hand as you worked on your project.

# Headings

It is customary to break up the text of a manuscript with headings. You can derive these from the outline of your term paper or, in the case of the research report, use the specific headings inherent in the structure of the report ("Introduction," "Method," and so on). Note how Maria's headings and subheadings lend symmetry to her paper, showing its progressive development in concise phrases:

Eating Disorders

Symptom-Oriented Approach

Behavior Therapy

Organic Procedures

Context-Oriented Approach

Overview and Examples

Subtleties of Group or Family Therapy

Conclusion

Maria's term paper uses two formats of headings: center and flush left. The **center heading** is used to separate the manuscript into major sections and is written in uppercase and lowercase letters and not underlined. To subdivide the major sections, she uses **subheadings** placed at the left margin (flush left), underlined, and in uppercase and lowercase. If we wished to use another level of subheadings, they would be indented, underlined, and followed by a period, with the body of the text immediately following the heading, for example:

<u>Nature of the Problem</u>

    <u>Definition.</u> Anorexia nervosa refers to . . .

# Underlining

As this example shows, **underlining** can be used to distinguish levels of headings. Conventional usage also calls for the titles of books mentioned in the body of the text to be underlined ("In <u>Pygmalion in the Classroom</u>, Rosenthal and Jacobson . . ."). Underlining is also used in several other ways:

➤ Letters used as statistical symbols are underlined: $\underline{F}$, $\underline{N}$, $\underline{n}$, $\underline{P}$, $\underline{p}$, $\underline{t}$, $\underline{z}$, and so forth. Incidentally, avoid capitalizing $\underline{t}$ if you mean Student's $\underline{t}$ test, because a capital letter implies a quite different statistic.

➤ However, Greek letters used as statistical symbols are not underlined, for example, the symbol for chi-square ($\chi^2$), the symbol telling us to sum a set of scores ($\Sigma$), the symbol for the standard deviation of a set of scores ($\sigma$), or the symbol for the variance of a set of scores ($\sigma^2$).

➤ In reference lists, the volume numbers of journal articles and the titles of books and journals are underlined.

➤ Words that you wish to emphasize are underlined, but this should be done sparingly ("Effective teaching, the authors assert, will come only from the teachers' firm belief that their pupils <u>can</u> perform . . .").

# Citations in Text

There are several simple conventions for citing an author's work in the narrative of a paper. The purpose of a citation is to make it easy for the reader to identify the source of a quotation or idea and then to locate that particular reference in the list at the end of the paper. The author-date method is the format generally recommended. The surname of the author and the year of publication are inserted in the narrative text at the appropriate point.

Here are three additional rules:

➤ Do not list any publication in your reference list that you do not cite.

➤ Do not cite any reference without placing it in the reference list.

➤ If you want to cite a source that you did not read, use the following format: "In Vergil's epic poem, the <u>Aeneid</u>, as quoted by Allport and Postman (1947), the following characterization of rumor appears: . . ." But do this only if the original source is unavailable to you; otherwise examine and cite the original source yourself.

In general, there are two categories of citations in student research reports and term papers (you will find many examples of each in Maria's and John's papers). One category consists of citations that appear as part of the narrative; the other category consists of citations inserted in alphabetical order (and then by year if the same author is cited twice) entirely in parentheses within the narrative.

## Citation Appearing as Part of Narrative

Kimmel, Govern, and Keefer (1991) asked a sample of psychologists to give their opinions about the ethical costs and benefits of various studies.

## Citation Entirely in Parentheses

Certain results raise the suspicion that members of peer review boards may harbor different biases regarding the costs and benefits of the studies they are asked to evaluate (e.g., Ceci, Peters, & Plotkin, 1985; Hamsher & Reznikoff, 1967; Kallgren & Kenrick, 1990; Schlenker & Forsyth, 1977).

These examples also illustrate the convention of author-date citations that dictates the listing of the surnames of all authors the first time the citation is given. However, in subsequent citations, if there are more than two authors, you mention the surname of only the first author, followed by *et al.* and the date, for example:

## Subsequent Citation as Part of Narrative

Ceci et al. (1985) reported that the identical research proposal, approved without changes in one institution, was amended at another institution in the same city.

## Subsequent Citation Entirely in Parentheses

It has been reported that the identical research proposal, approved without changes in one institution, was amended at another institution in the same city (Ceci et al., 1985).

Notice that in the pair of citations on page 75 the word *and* is spelled out in the narrative citation but that an ampersand (&) is used in the parenthetical citation. This is conventional usage in psychology and many related areas. Here are some other specific rules that cover most simple cases:

➤ If you are citing a series of works, the proper sequence is by alphabetical order of the surname of the first author and then by chronological order: (Crabb, 1990; DiFonzo & Bordia, 1993; Fung, 1989, 1990; Gergen & Shotter, 1985, 1988; Jaeger, 1975, 1980; Stern, in press; Strohmetz, 1991, 1992).

➤ Two works published by the same author in the same year are designated *a, b, c,* and so on: (Baenninger & LoSciuto, 1993a, 1993b, 1993c). In the reference list, the alphabetical order of the works' titles determines sequence when there is more than one work by the author in the same year.

➤ Work accepted for publication but not yet printed is designated "in press": (Hesson, in press); in a list of citations, the rule is to place this work last: (Hesson, 1985, 1986, in press).

What should you do if you run into a problem that these rules do not address? If your instructor is a stickler for the APA style of handling citations, then look in the most recent edition of the *Publication Manual of the American Psychological Association.* We are not sticklers and recommend only that you keep one general idea in mind as you reach within these specific guidelines: **If you run into a problem, use common sense.** Ask yourself whether you yourself could find the one reference referred to based on the citation you have provided. In other words, put yourself in your reader's shoes.

# Tables and Figures

As with the title page (and the abstract of the research report), present each table and figure on a separate sheet of paper. Often, when students include tables in their research reports, the instructor finds that they are merely presenting their raw data in a neat format. Save your raw data for the appendix of your report (if your raw data are required), and keep in mind that statistical tables in research reports are **summaries** of raw data (see Table 2 of John's report) and other results.

As John's report illustrates, a table is placed on a separate page and inserted just after the page on which it is first introduced in the narrative. To make it easy for the reader to locate, John states, "Examples of these two kinds of rumors are listed in Table 1 (see page 8)." Notice that on page 8 of John's paper the title is shown above the table, and all information in the table is double-spaced.

It is also possible to use a **figure,** which is any type of exhibit or illustration other than a table. An easy way to differentiate between tables and figures is to think of tables in journal articles as typeset but figures as photographed from artwork. Had John used a figure to illustrate the information in his Table 2, it might have looked like this:

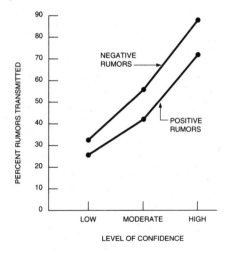

Figure 1. Transmission rate as a function of low, moderate, and high confidence in truth of negative and positive rumors.

Observe that the caption (the title of the figure) goes below the figure, and that it begins with an uppercase letter and ends with a period. If you are working with a graphics program, you can compose the figure on the computer. The basic rule is to use figures that add to the text; do not simply repeat what you can say very clearly in words. Two informative and entertaining books on the development of graphics are *The Visual Display of Quantitative Information* and *Envisioning Information*, both by Edward R. Tufte (Graphics Press). As Tufte points out, sometimes elaborate figures introduce distortions, thus detracting from a clear, concise summary of the data. Be sure not to overcomplicate your figure; try it out on a friend to see whether he or she understands it.

However you choose to display your findings in the research report, the title or caption must be clearly and precisely stated. If you need to add some clarifying or explanatory note to your table, it is customary to place this information below the table in a note, for example:

Note. The possible range of scores was from 1 (strong disagreement) to 5 (strong agreement), with 3 indicating no opinion.

If you want to make specific notes, the convention is to use superscript lowercase letters ($^{a\,b\,c}$) or asterisks (\* \*\* \*\*\*). The following cases illustrate this usage:

## Superscript Notation

$^{a}\underline{n} = 50$     $^{b}\underline{n} = 62$

## Asterisk Notation

\*$\underline{p} < .05$     \*\*$\underline{p} < .01$     \*\*\*$\underline{p} < .005$

The following guidelines will prove helpful if you are preparing a figure.

➤ The figure should be neat, clearly presented, and precisely labeled to augment your discussion.
➤ The figure should be large enough to read easily.
➤ The units should progress from small to large.
➤ The data should be precisely plotted. If you are drawing the figure by hand, use graph paper to help you keep the rows and columns evenly spaced.

➤ When graphing the relationship between an independent variable and a dependent variable (or between a predictor variable and a criterion variable), it is customary to put the independent (or predictor) variable on the horizontal axis and the dependent (or criterion) variable on the vertical axis.

One exception to the last convention is the stem-and-leaf display, described in many textbooks on research methods and basic statistics. The beauty of the stem-and-leaf format is that it preserves the original numbers yet manages to give an economical summary of them. (For an advanced discussion, see John W. Tukey's *Exploratory Data Analysis,* published by Addison-Wesley.)

# Reference List

The reference list starts on a new page. The references are arranged alphabetically by the surname of the author(s) and then by the date of publication. The standard style is to

➤ Invert all authors' names (that is, last name, first name, middle initial).
➤ List the authors' names in the exact order in which they appear on the title page of the publication.
➤ Use commas to separate the authors and an ampersand (&) before the last author.
➤ Give the year the work was copyrighted (the year and month for magazine articles and the year, month, and day for newspaper articles).
➤ For book titles, capitalize only the first word of the title and of the subtitle (if any), as well as any proper names.
➤ For journal titles, capitalize the first word of the title and of the subtitle (if any), as well as all other words except coordinating conjunctions (such as *and* and *or*), articles (*a, an,* and *the*), and prepositions (such as *in, of,* and *for*).
➤ Give the issue number of the journal if the article cited is paginated by issue.
➤ Underline the volume number and name of a journal and the title of a book.
➤ Give the city of a book's publisher.

➤ If the city is not well known or might be confused with another location (for instance, Cambridge, Massachusetts, and Cambridge, England), give the state (or country).

➤ When in doubt about whether to list the state, list it.

➤ Use the postal abbreviation for the state, for instance, MA for "Massachusetts."

Using these pointers, the examples in Maria's and John's papers, and the following examples as general guidelines, you should encounter no problems. If you do run into one, however, the rule of thumb is to be clear, consistent, and complete in listing your source material.

## Authored Book

Kimmel, A. J. (1988). Ethics and values in applied social research. Newbury Park, CA: Sage.

Lana, R. E. (1969). Assumptions of social psychology. New York: Appleton-Century-Crofts.

Levin, J., & Arluke, A. (1987). Gossip: The inside scoop. New York: Plenum.

## Work in Press (edited volume, journal article, authored book)

Blanck, P. D. (Ed.). (in press). Interpersonal expectations: Theory, research, and applications. New York: Cambridge University Press.

Fine, G. A. (in press). The city as a folklore generator: Urban legends in the metropolis. Urban Resources.

Kapferer, J. (in press). Rumors: Uses, interpretations, and images. New Brunswick, NJ: Transaction Publishers.

## Edited Published Work

Gergen, K. J., & Gergen, M. (Eds.). (1984). Historical social psychology. Hillsdale, NJ: Erlbaum.

Morawski, J. G. (Ed.). (1988). The rise of experimentation in American psychology. New Haven: Yale University Press.

## Work Republished at a Later Date

Demosthenes. (1852). The Olynthiac and other public orations of Demosthenes. London: Henry G. Bohn. (Original work written 349 B.C.)

Lessing, G. E. (1779/1971). Gotthold Ephraim Lessing: Werke (Vol. 2). Munich: Carl Hanser Verlag.

Pope, A. (1733/1903). Moral essays: Epistle I. To Sir Richard Temple, Lord Cobham, of the knowledge and character of men. In H. W. Boynton (Ed.), The complete poetical works of Pope (pp. 157–160). Boston: Houghton Mifflin.

## Journal Article Paginated by Volume (Three Authors)

Arms, R. L., Russell, G. W., & Sandilands, M. L. (1979). Effects on the hostility of spectators' viewing aggressive sports. Social Psychology Quarterly, 42, 275–279.

Tybout, A. M., Calder, B. J., & Sternthal, B. (1981). Using information processing theory to design marketing strategies. Journal of Marketing Research, 18, 73–79.

## Article Paginated by Issue

Goldstein, J. H. (1978). In vivo veritas: Has humor research looked at humor? Humor Research Newsletter, 3(1), 3–4.

Valdiserri, R. O., Tama, G. M., & Ho, M. (1988). The role of community advisory committees in clinical trials of anti-HIV agents. IRB: A Review of Human Subjects Research, 10(4), 5–7.

## Article in Foreign Language (Title Translated into English)

Foa, U. G. (1966). Le nombre huit dans la socialization de l'enfant [The number eight in the socialization of the infant]. Bulletin du Centre d'Etudes et Recherches Psychologiques, 15, 39–47.

Jung, C. G. (1910). Ein Beitrag zur Psychologie des Gerüchtes [A contribution on the psychology of rumor]. Zentralblatt für Psychoanalyse, 1, 81–90.

## Chapter in Multivolume Edited Series

Kipnis, D. (1984). The use of power in organizations and interpersonal settings. In S. Oskamp (Ed.), Applied social psychology (Vol. 5, pp. 171–210). Newbury Park, CA: Sage.

Koch, S. (1959). General introduction to the series. In S. Koch (Ed.), Psychology: A study of a science (Vol. 1, pp. 1–18). New York: McGraw-Hill.

## Magazine or Newspaper Article

Rowan, R. (1979, August 13). Where did that rumor come from? Fortune, pp. 130–137.

Sexton, J. (1990, January 14). Rumors have effect on Rangers. The New York Times, Section 8, pp. 1, 4.

## Doctoral Dissertation Abstract

Esposito, J. (1987). Subjective factors and rumor transmission: A field investigation of the influence of anxiety, importance, and belief on rumormongering (doctoral dissertation, Temple University, 1986). Dissertation Abstracts International, 48, 596B.

## Technical Report

Kipnis, D., & Kidder, L. H. (1977). Practice performance and sex: Sex role appropriateness, success and failure as determinants of men's and women's task learning capabilities (Report No. 1). Philadelphia: University City Science Center.

## Unpublished Manuscript

Kimmel, A. J., & Keefer, R. (1989). Psychological correlates of the acceptance and transmission of rumors about AIDS. Unpublished manuscript, Fitchburg State College, Department of Behavioral Science, Fitchburg, MA.

## Paper Presented at a Meeting

Lamberth, J. (1981, January). Jury selection: A psychological approach. Paper presented at the meeting of the American Trial Association, Moorestown, NJ.

## Poster Presented at a Meeting

Walker, C. J., & Blaine, B. E. (1989, April). The virulence of dread rumors: A field experiment. Poster presented at the meeting of the Eastern Psychological Association, Boston.

# Proofing and Correcting

We now come to the final steps before you submit your paper: proofing and correcting. Read the finished manuscript more than once. Ask yourself the following questions:

➤ Are there omissions?
➤ Are there misspellings?

➤ Are the numbers correct?

➤ Are the hyphenations correct?

➤ Are all the references cited in the body of the paper listed in the references section?

The first time you read your final draft, the appeal of the neat, clean copy can lead you to overlook errors. Put the paper aside for 24 hours and then read it carefully again. If you find errors, correct them before you submit the finished product. If you typed the paper and find small mistakes, use correction fluid to cover them and make the required corrections. Do not just type over an incorrect letter or number. If you typed the paper and find a substantial omission or many such omissions, retype the entire page.

Give your paper a final look, checking to be sure all the pages are there and in order. If you adhered to the guidelines in this manual, you should have a sense of a job well done and feel confident that the paper will receive the serious attention that a clear, consistent, and attractive manuscript deserves.

# Sample Term Paper

Therapeutic Orientations in the Treatment

of Anorexia Nervosa


Maria Di Medio




Term Paper

(Number and Name of Course)

Instructor: (Name)

(Date Submitted)

2

## Abstract

Anorexia nervosa refers to an eating disorder characterized by a preoccupation with being overweight, even though the person is underweight, and a refusal to maintain normal body weight.  Two therapeutic orientations are discussed.  One approach induces weight gain by using behavioral or organic procedures, and the second approach induces weight gain but also emphasizes social factors by employing group or family therapy.  Examples and representative problems are described, and it is concluded that the latter approach is more generally recommended in treating anorexia nervosa.

3

Eating Disorders

In a society in which food is plentiful and indeed a topic
of almost obsessive interest and concern, it seems paradoxical
that an eating disorder can be so prevalent. Anorexia nervosa
is such a disorder. It is traditionally defined as "a serious
nervous condition in which the patient loses his [her] appetite
and systematically takes but little food, so that he [she]
becomes greatly emaciated" (<u>Dorland's Medical Dictionary</u>, 1957,
p. 94). The word <u>anorexia</u> comes from the Greek "want of
appetite," and <u>nervosa</u> indicates a nervous condition. More
recently, the syndrome has been expanded to include the symptom
that anorectic individuals have (along with emaciation) the
problem of depression (Halmi, Eckert, LaDu, & Cohen, 1986).
Patients also are described as having a distorted body image;
that is, they perceive themselves as layered in fat even when
they are noticeably underweight. Typically, anorectic patients
(the majority of whom are women) starve themselves to attain
dramatic weight loss and refuse to maintain normal body weight
(Edelstein, 1989).

This nervous disorder can be differentiated from other
subclasses of eating disorders such as bulimia nervosa and
pica. <u>Bulimics</u> are individuals who "binge eat," or consume
large amounts of food. Interestingly, anorexia and bulimia can
be associated, such as when patients with anorexia nervosa have
episodes of eating binges followed by self-induced vomiting
(<u>bulimia nervosa</u>). It is a dangerous pattern because it can
result in depletion of vital nutritional elements and thus lead

4

to death.  Pica, another subclass of eating disorders, refers to "a craving for unnatural articles of food" (Dorland's Medical Dictionary, 1957, p. 1053), and sometimes appears in pregnant women.

There are, of course, several other recognizable types of eating disorders (American Psychiatric Association, 1987), but in this term paper I will concentrate on what I perceive as two general orientations in the treatment of anorexia nervosa.  One approach (which I characterize as symptom-oriented) focuses on inducing weight gain using behavioral or organic procedures.  A second approach (characterized here as context-oriented) emphasizes weight gain but also focuses on social factors by employing group or family therapy.  Examples of each are noted, and representative problems are described.  On the basis of this limited review, I conclude that the context-oriented approach is more generally recommended in the treatment of anorexia nervosa.

### Symptom-Oriented Approach

In this approach, the sole emphasis is on treatment of the symptom of significant weight loss.  One subclass of procedures employs behavior therapy (e.g., operant conditioning, desensitization), while another subclass uses organic procedures (e.g., force feeding, also called hyperalimentation, and drugs).  In some cases, both procedures have been employed in the same treatment regimen.

Behavior Therapy

In an early example, a 37-year-old anorectic patient weighed only 47 pounds when operant conditioning treatment was begun

## 5

(Bachrach, Erwin, & Mohr, 1965). Initially, she was deprived of any positive reinforcements (e.g., music, visitors). She then ate her meals in the presence of a psychologist, medical student, or resident, who reinforced her verbally whenever she made an effort to eat. Eventually, evidence of weight gain became the criterion for reinforcement. The patient's family continued reinforcing her efforts to eat, and by the end of the program the patient weighed 88 pounds. However, a follow-up study, 14 years later, revealed that this patient's weight had dropped to 55 pounds, a result of her not getting sufficient amounts of food (Erwin, 1977). Despite her precarious weight, the patient's social life had improved as she became involved in outside activities.

Another early study, however, reported little difference in the results of operant conditioning in hospital patients who were subjected to behavior modification and other patients who did not receive behavior modification (Eckert, Goldberg, Halmi, Casper, & Davis, 1979).

Systematic desensitization is another behavioral procedure in the treatment of anorexia. It focuses on the anxiety associated with eating and establishes a hierarchy for the specific fear-eliciting stimuli (e.g., travel, disapproval, insecurity). In one early example, desensitization was used with a 23-year-old woman who had rapidly lost 20 pounds and displayed anxiety about eating (Lang, 1965). She often did not eat when she was in new surroundings or at odds with someone. During desensitization she was offered candy, but although she

6

was desensitized, her problem could not be remediated.  However, her repeated refusal to eat has also been explained as a reaction to stress rather than an obsessive preoccupation with weight loss.

Critics argue that the behavioral approach is problematic at best.  The weight gain achieved is short-lived, they maintain, as the underlying psychological problems are left untreated (e.g., Bruch, 1979).  Depriving anorectic patients of privileges is also viewed by critics as of questionable value (Bemis, 1978).  Some other perennial concerns are that small numbers of patients have been used in evaluative studies, and the effects of treatment are often confounded because of the simultaneous administration of multiple medications to the patients (Eckert et al., 1979).

<u>Organic Procedures</u>

Hyperalimentation (tube feeding) and drug therapy are two organic procedures that have also been used in the treatment of anorexia nervosa.  Lithium carbonate has been found to increase the patient's intake of fatty foods and thus produce weight gain (Gross, Evert, Goldberg, Faden, Nee, & Kaye, 1980).  It is not known how this drug directly influences weight, but it may have an effect on glucose metabolism (which affects one's desire to eat).  Typically, those treated with the drug do not deny their illness as much as those who do not receive the drug.  Despite the weight gain associated with use of this drug, the procedure has been criticized on grounds that the patient's psychological well-being is not considered (Andersen, 1979; Bemis, 1978).  In

7

addition, lithium can produce physical problems with anorectic patients, who may show signs of dehydration, electrolyte imbalances, and impaired heart function (Mitchell & Eckert, 1987).

Antidepressants (such as amitriptyline) have been tested on anorectic subjects, but their effects on inducing weight gain seem to be questionable (Mitchell & Eckert, 1987). One study reported that amitriptyline promoted weight gain for bulimic anorectic patients (Halmi et al., 1986). However, the bulimic anorectic subjects also reported higher pretreatment levels of depression than subjects with only anorexia, which might account for the effectiveness of amitriptyline with the bulimic subgroup. Andersen (1987) recommended using antidepressants only for anorectic patients who also suffered from depression but not the use of antidepressants as a means of inducing weight gain.

The drug cyproheptadine (an antihistaminic, antipruritic) has been employed as an appetite stimulant with anorectic patients (Goldberg, Halmi, Eckert, Casper, & Davis, 1979; Halmi et al., 1986). Goldberg et al. (1979) noted that cyproheptadine promoted the most weight gain among anorectic subjects who had previous treatment failures and who had a history of complications at birth (e.g., respiratory problems, breech birth). In a study comparing cyproheptadine, amitriptyline, and a placebo, Halmi et al. (1986) found that anorectic individuals without bulimic symptoms benefited most from cyproheptadine. However, there were also significant differences in treatment

8

effectiveness in the three hospitals used in this study.  It is
possible, then, that hospital setting is a confounding factor in
this study (e.g., influencing the subjects' cooperativeness or
some other relevant motivational variable).

Context-Oriented Approach

In this approach, the aim is to treat weight loss symptoms
while also concentrating on social factors.  Variations of
psychotherapy have been used to bolster the organic procedures
involved in effecting weight gain.  For example, the family's
relationship with the anorectic patient comes under scrutiny
when family therapy is used to address underlying problems.

<u>Overview and Examples</u>

What appears to be the most effective treatment for anorexia
nervosa involves the establishment of a weight gain regimen
accompanied or followed by psychotherapy for the patient and
family members.  One hypothesis is that anorectic individuals
are perfectionists who strive to please the standards (real or
imagined) of their families.  An alternative hypothesis is that
the behavior of patients is an attempt to manipulate their
families in order to gain control over their own lives.  Various
combinations of weight gain treatments with psychotherapy have
been tried (Geller, 1975; Maloney & Farrell, 1980).

Interestingly, one study reported success with a behavioral
method of individual therapy (Geller, 1975).  A 22-year-old
woman not only gained weight but also reported feeling more in
control of her body after therapy.  She was capable of
expressing her feelings about eating more openly.  Long-term

9

results were not reported, however.  Hyperalimentation in combination with therapy has also proven effective in terms of weight gain, improved social behavior, enhanced concentration, and more facile expression of feelings (Maloney & Farrell, 1980).

Bruch (1979) recommended that weight gain precede therapy, and that therapy commence when the patient weighs approximately 90-95 pounds.  Another aspect of the recommended therapy was to dispel maladaptive distortions about eating, thereby enhancing the patient's ability to see how behavior adversely affects the body.  Once the patient attains a feeling of control over his or her body, it may be possible to generalize that feeling to other areas of life.

One integrated treatment approach (Andersen, 1987) starts out by stabilizing the patient's weight.  Once patients attain 85-90% of their ideal weight, then outpatient treatment begins. Patients receive intensive psychotherapy to help them deal with everyday problems.  Family therapy can be instituted to help family members support the anorectic patient in the treatment. Then, a maintenance program of the patient's weight begins, in which patients can choose their own food.  This program was effective with individuals who developed anorexia at an early age (before 18 years), had a stable personality, and also had a stable family life before the onset of anorexia.

Garner (1987) has outlined an integrative program for the use of cognitive therapy.  First, the patient gains weight in a hospital setting in conjunction with receiving information about

10

starvation and weight regulation.  Once the patient has reached
75% of pre-anorexia weight, outpatient therapy begins.  In
cognitive therapy, the psychotherapist challenges the distorted
beliefs and thoughts of the anorexic.  For instance, patients
may tend to engage in all-or-none thinking (e.g., "I'm too fat
if I gain 5 pounds") and overgeneralization of failures (e.g.,
"I'm a failure as a person because this boy doesn't like me").
The therapist reasons with the patient and assigns homework to
convert the patient's thinking to a more realistic world view.

Subtleties of Group or Family Therapy

Hall (1985) observed that group therapy with anorectic
subjects can be difficult because patients tend to be
withdrawn.  Hall also provided some guidelines for increasing
the likelihood of success in group therapy.  For instance, it
was observed that a warm, flexible therapist who can facilitate
expression of feelings can promote group cohesiveness.  Hall
recommended that anorectic patients be induced to gain weight
before beginning group therapy.

In family therapy, the patient's role in the family and the
attitudes of family members are taken into consideration.  The
patient may undergo behavior modification to change eating
patterns.  Then, after the family has met with the professionals
involved in the case, all parties (including the patient) engage
in a luncheon session.  It is structured so that the family's
response to the patient's eating problem may be strongly
disapproving (e.g., badgering the patient about eating habits)
or, at the other extreme, the family may overlook the problem

11

(i.e., pretend it does not exist). Some families have been reported to be reluctant to undertake these modes of treatment, concerned that long-buried family conflicts might erupt. Out of 53 patients, 86% were reported as being treated effectively by family therapy (Minuchin, Rosman, & Baker, 1978).

A recent evaluation of family therapy for anorectic patients compared it with individual therapy (Russell, Dare, Eisler, & LeGrange, 1992). The study reported that younger anorectic subjects or those who showed symptoms for fewer than three years benefited the most from family therapy. Individual therapy worked better for older patients. Perhaps families exert a stronger influence on younger patients, thereby making family therapy more effective in treating such cases. Russell et al. recommended that family therapy should not emphasize family pathology, because family members then become defensive. Family therapy should focus on parents' monitoring their child's eating behavior, not on implying that any family members are responsible for causing the disorder.

Conclusion

In this term paper I have described two general therapeutic orientations in the treatment of anorexia nervosa. One approach was characterized as symptom-oriented and the other as context-oriented, although there was clearly some overlap between these two categories. Based on this sampling of relevant work, I conclude that the context-oriented approach is more generally recommended. By addressing not only the patient's eating habits but also focusing on the social setting (i.e., the context of

12

underlying conflicts), a more efficacious outcome seems to be
predicted.

13

References

American Psychiatric Association (1987). <u>Diagnostic and</u>
<u>statistical manual of mental disorders</u> (3rd ed.). Washington,
DC: Author.

Andersen, A. E. (1979). Anorexia nervosa: Diagnosis and
treatment. <u>Weekly Psychiatry Update Series</u> (Rep. 3).
Princeton, NJ: Biomedia.

Andersen, A. E. (1987). Inpatient and outpatient treatment of
anorexia nervosa. In K. D. Brownell & J. P. Foreyt (Eds.),
<u>Handbook of eating disorders</u> (pp. 333-350). New York: Basic
Books.

Bachrach, A., Erwin, W., & Mohr, J. (1965). The control of
eating behavior in an anorectic by operant conditioning
techniques. In L. P. Ullman & L. Krasner (Eds.), <u>Case studies</u>
<u>in behavior modification</u> (pp. 153-163). New York: Holt,
Rinehart & Winston.

Bemis, K. (1978). Current approaches to the etiology and
treatment of anorexia nervosa. <u>Psychological Bulletin</u>, <u>85</u>,
593-617.

Bruch, H. (1979). <u>The golden cage: The enigma of anorexia</u>
<u>nervosa</u>. New York: Vintage.

<u>Dorland's medical dictionary</u>. (1957). Philadelphia: Saunders.

Eckert, E., Goldberg, S., Halmi, K., Casper, R., & Davis, J.
(1979). Behavior therapy in anorexia nervosa. <u>British</u>
<u>Journal of Psychiatry</u>, <u>134</u>, 55-59.

Edelstein, E. L. (1989). <u>Anorexia nervosa and other dyscontrol</u>
<u>disorders</u>. Berlin: Springer-Verlag.

14

Erwin, W. (1977). A 16 yrs. follow up case of severe anorexia
nervosa. Journal of Behavior and Experimental Psychiatry, 84,
157-160.

Garner, D. M. (1987). Cognitive therapy for anorexia nervosa. In
K. D. Brownell & J. P. Foreyt (Eds.), Handbook of eating
disorders (pp. 301-325). New York: Basic Books.

Geller, J. (1975). Treatment of anorexia nervosa by the
integration of behavior therapy and psychotherapy.
Psychotherapy and Psychosomatics, 26, 167-177.

Goldberg, S. C., Halmi, K. A., Eckert, E. D., Casper, R. C., &
Davis, J. M. (1979). Cyproheptadine in anorexia nervosa.
British Journal of Psychiatry, 134, 67-70.

Gross, H., Evert, M., Goldberg, S., Faden, V., Nee, L., & Kaye,
W. (1980). A double blind controlled trial of lithium
carbonate in primary anorexia nervosa. Unpublished
manuscript, National Institute of Mental Health Clinical
Center, Bethesda, MD.

Hall, A. (1985). Group psychotherapy for anorexia nervosa. In D.
M. Garner and P. E. Garfinkel (Eds.), Handbook of
psychotherapy for anorexia nervosa and bulimia (pp. 213-238).
New York: Guilford.

Halmi, K. A., Eckert, E., LaDu, T. J., & Cohen, J. (1986).
Anorexia nervosa: Treatment efficacy of cyproheptadine and
amitriptyline. Archives in General Psychiatry, 43, 177-181.

Lang, P. (1965). Behavior therapy with a case of nervous
anorexia. In L. Ullman & L. Krasner (Eds.), Case studies in

15

behavior modification (pp. 217-221). New York: Holt, Rinehart
& Winston.

Maloney, M., & Farrell, M. (1980). Treatment of severe weight
loss in anorexia nervosa with hyperalimentation and
psychotherapy. American Journal of Psychiatry, 137, 314-318.

Minuchin, S., Rosman, B., & Baker, L. (1978). Psychosomatic
families: Anorexia nervosa in context. Cambridge, MA: Harvard
University Press.

Mitchell, J., & Eckert, E. D. (1987). Scope and significance of
eating disorders. Journal of Consulting and Clinical
Psychology, 55, 628-634.

Russell, G. F. M., Dare, C., Eisler, I., & LeGrange, P. D. F.
(1992). Controlled trials of family treatments in anorexia
nervosa. In K. A. Halmi (Ed.), Psychobiology and treatment
of anorexia nervosa and bulimia nervosa (pp. 237-261).
Washington, DC: American Psychopathological Association.

# APPENDIX B

# Sample Research Report

Confidence in Rumor and the Likelihood of Transmission:

A Correlational Study

John H. Yost

Research Report

(Number and Name of Course)

Instructor: (Name)

(Date Submitted)

2

## Abstract

Tense labor negotiations provided a setting of anxiety in which
to study the transmission of rumors. Were individuals more
likely to transmit rumors when they were confident of the truth
of the rumor? This question was addressed to faculty members in
the midst of labor negotiations between the union and university
administration. Participants were asked to complete a
questionnaire in which they reported any rumors that they had
heard concerning the ongoing negotiations, to state whether or
not they had transmitted the rumors, and to rate their
confidence in the truth of the rumors. As hypothesized, there
was a positive linear relationship between the amount of
confidence and the likelihood of transmission of the rumor. The
results are discussed in the context of recent rumor theory.

## 3

## Introduction

The psychology of rumor has for many years fascinated poets and social scientists. In their classic work, <u>The Psychology of Rumor</u>, Allport and Postman (1947, epigraph) quoted the following lines from Vergil's <u>Aeneid</u>:

Swift through the Libyan cities Rumor sped.

Rumor! What evil can surpass her speed?

In movement she grows mighty, and achieves

Strength and dominion as she swifter flies.

Small first, because afraid, she soon exalts

Her stature skyward, stalking through the lands

And mantling in the clouds her baleful brow...

These ancient lines have a contemporary ring to them, but many of Allport and Postman's original assertions about the factors that give rise to rumor or influence its subsequent development no longer strike a resonant chord (e.g., Buckner, 1965; Esposito & Rosnow, 1984). The problem is that many of Allport and Postman's speculations, although plausible, have failed to generate scientific support. As a consequence, there have been attempts to formulate a more empirically grounded understanding of the psychology of rumor (e.g., Festinger, Cartwright, Barber, Fleischl, Gottsdanker, Keysen, & Leavitt, 1948; Rosnow, 1980; Schachter & Burdick, 1955; Shibutani, 1966).

What is rumor, and what are the circumstances that stimulate its growth? Going back to Allport and Postman (1947), rumor has been traditionally defined in psychology as a proposition for belief that is unverified and in general circulation. A current

4

rumor theory (Rosnow, 1980) suggests that the amount of rumor in circulation is determined by a complex function of anxiety (an emotional factor) and uncertainty (a cognitive factor). These two conditions, when stimulated by ongoing events, are posited to be linearly related to rumor strength. That is, when a situation elicits little anxiety or uncertainty, the low levels of arousal should not generate rumors. However, when a situation elicits higher levels of anxiety and uncertainty, there is a more urgent desire to reduce the emotional and cognitive unrest. The greater the anxiety and uncertainty, the greater should be the need to alleviate discomfort.

Knapp (1944), a student of Allport's, observed that rumors thrive in periods of social stress. Current rumor theory is consistent with this observation, and different investigations of rumor concern periods of obvious discomfort, such as a catastrophe or a war (e.g., Knapp, 1944; Nkpa, 1975; Prasad, 1935), but none has actually collected data on the rate of rumor transmission. Data concerning the reasons individuals transmit certain rumors and not others would be valuable in helping to understand the phenomenon of rumormongering.

Why is it that some rumors are transmitted with greater alacrity than others during stressful situations? In this study it was hypothesized that the more confidence one has in the truth of a rumor, the more likely one is to transmit the rumor. This hypothesis proceeds on the assumption that the credibility of the person passing the rumor is at stake when a rumor is transmitted. It should be to one's advantage to communicate

5

information that has a good chance of being true rather than information that is likely to prove false. Passing false rumors might jeopardize one's future credibility, while passing rumors that prove true would enhance one's future credibility.

There is already some experimental evidence that supports the idea of a relationship between confidence in rumor and rumor transmission. Jaeger, Anthony, and Rosnow (1980) planted a rumor among college students. In one condition the rumor was refuted by a confederate, and in another condition the rumor was not refuted. Subjects in the refutation groups reported lower initial belief in the rumor than subjects in the nonrefutation groups, and the rumor was circulated with lower frequency when refuted. The present study sought to determine whether this relationship found in an experimental setting with college students also held true in a field setting with a different population of subjects. The question addressed was whether there was a significant positive relationship between confidence in the truth of rumors and rumor transmission during a period of stressful labor negotiations.

Method

In this study, rumors were collected during a stressful period. A university community was divided over contract negotiations between the faculty union and the university administration. The faculty union had voted to strike if a contract agreement was not reached by a specific deadline. Publicly, the administration refused to negotiate on the faculty union's major demand. The university community was gripped with

6

tension as the strike deadline approached.  There was much
speculation as to whether or not there would be a strike as well
as what to do should a strike occur.  The data in this study
were collected in the week prior to the strike deadline, when
tensions seemed relatively high.  Only a last-minute settlement
averted a strike, and most members of the university community
were unclear about the situation until the final moments.

Questionnaires were placed in the interoffice mailboxes of
505 full-time faculty members from 28 different departments one
morning, 10 days before the strike deadline that had been
announced by the union.  The instructions asked the recipients
to list any rumors they had heard over the past several days
that pertained to ongoing labor negotiations at the university.
Rumor was defined as "any report, statement, or story that one
may have heard or mentioned for which there is no immediate
evidence available to verify its truth."  After reporting each
rumor the respondents were asked to indicate whether or not they
had subsequently transmitted the rumor and to rate their
confidence in the truth of the rumor on a 0 to 10 scale.  Zero
represented "no confidence in the truth of the rumor" and 10
represented "strong confidence in the truth of the rumor."
Anonymity was assured, and the participants were asked to return
the completed questionnaire through the interoffice mail within
7 days (3 days before the strike deadline).  There were 55
questionnaires returned, for a response rate of 11 percent.

Results

In these 55 questionnaires there were 134 responses that

were purported to be "rumors" by the respondents. The 134 items were classified by two independent raters as positive rumors, negative rumors, or nonrumors. There were 20 items that were classified as nonrumors, leaving a total of 114 rumors. Rumors were classified as "positive" if the judges agreed that the outcome of the rumor would be beneficial to the respondent (i.e., beneficial to faculty members). Rumors were classified as "negative" if the judges agreed that the outcome of the rumor would be detrimental to the respondent (i.e., detrimental to faculty members). Examples of these two kinds of rumors are listed in Table 1 (see page 8). Of the 114 rumors reported, 22 were classified as positive and 92 as negative.

Within both positive and negative categories, the confidence ratings were collapsed to form three levels of confidence: low (ratings of 0 to 3), moderate (4 to 6), and high (7 to 10). The results are shown in Table 2 (see page 9) in terms of the percentage of positive and negative rumors reported as having been transmitted by the respondent at each of the three levels of confidence. I analyzed these results for linearity, but it should be noted that the frequencies within cells cannot actually be viewed as independent (i.e., there were more rumors than subjects). Still, it is clearly evident that there was an increasing linear relationship between the confidence in the rumor and its transmission rate. A linear trend analysis, employing the contrast procedure (for independent data) described by Rosenthal and Rosnow (1985), was used to analyze these results.

8

Table 1

Sample Rumors

---

<u>Positive rumors</u>

"Even if there were to be a strike, the faculty would not lose
any pay."

"The administration is ready to settle."

<u>Negative rumors</u>

"The administration wants a strike to break the union."

"All faculty benefits will be stopped if a strike occurs; also,
salaries will be stopped."

---

9

Table 2

Rates of Transmission of Rumors

| Confidence | Negative Rumors (%) | Positive Rumors (%) |
|------------|---------------------|---------------------|
| High       | 86.1                | 71.4                |
| Moderate   | 52.4                | 42.9                |
| Low        | 31.4                | 25.0                |

10

For negative rumors, the linear contrast $\underline{Z}$ was highly significant ($\underline{Z}$ = 5.67, $\underline{p}$ = .00000001 one-tailed); the effect size was also impressive ($\underline{r}$ = .59). For positive rumors, the results were not as exciting statistically, but were impressive nonetheless, with $\underline{Z}$ = 2.00, $\underline{p}$ = .02 one-tailed, $\underline{r}$ = .43. Although these results cannot be taken as proof of causality, they are consistent with the idea that individuals are more inclined to pass rumors they believe than rumors they do not believe.

Discussion

The findings are consistent with current rumor theory, which asserts that when a situation elicits high anxiety and uncertainty there is a more urgent desire to reduce the emotional and cognitive discomfort. This desire to alleviate discomfort will often result in rumor transmission when individuals are trying to make sense of a situation and to assess possible future outcomes. If someone has low confidence in the truth of a rumor, upon transmission this person's anxiety and uncertainty may not decrease. It may even increase because of the added stress of transmitting information that may be false and potentially damaging to one's credibility. Therefore, individuals may have a tendency not to pass a rumor when they do not have much confidence in its veracity. On the other hand, the more confidence people have in the truth of a rumor, the more effective will be the alleviation of discomfort as they transmit the rumor. Even if it serves only to verify a problem, the rumor provides a basis for making plans to confront the

11

troubling situation.

In other words, for positive rumors the alleviation of discomfort may be a reinforcement of an expected outcome of a rumor. The uneasiness of "getting one's hopes up only to be later disappointed" is alleviated. For example, if a faculty member hears that the strike will not occur and has confidence in the truth of this rumor, the rumor may be transmitted to alleviate stress. Feedback from others that supports the belief tends to reassure the person and minimize the discomfort brought on by uncertainty and anxiety. For negative rumors, the alleviation of discomfort may come in the form of a plan to cope with the predicted consequences of the rumor. For example, if an individual has confidence in a rumor that states there will be a strike, the person may transmit the rumor in order to assess what to do in case of a strike.

Rumors can also provide social sanctions for those passing them to say negative things about others (Knapp, 1944). If one is sure of the truth of a rumor, the discomfort stemming from the situation will be alleviated and the usual social taboos will be less likely to come into play. In this study, 25% of all negative rumors (20% of all rumors) were hostile; they assigned the blame for an imminent strike to the president of the university or the administration. This is analogous to a worker who dislikes a manager saying hostile things about the manager through rumors, which is a normatively acceptable form of disparagement during a stressful situation. In this way, rumors may have a purging effect.

12

  Further investigation is warranted to see if the findings in this study can be generalized to other naturalistic settings. It is also essential that sources of confounding in this study be controlled in future research.  With reports of rumors continuing to proliferate recently in the stock market (Wiggins, 1985) and the business world (Koenig, 1985), additional research on the topic is clearly needed.

13

References

Allport, G. W., & Postman, L. (1947). <u>The psychology of rumor</u>.
New York: Holt, Rinehart & Winston.

Buckner, H. T. (1965). A theory of rumor transmission. <u>Public
Opinion Quarterly</u>, <u>29</u>, 54-70.

Esposito, J. L., & Rosnow, R. L. (1984). Cognitive set and
message processing: Implications of prose memory research for
rumor theory. <u>Language and Communication</u>, <u>4</u>, 301-315.

Festinger, L., Cartwright, D., Barber, K., Fleischl, J.,
Gottsdanker, J., Keysen, A., & Leavitt, G. (1948). A study of
rumor: Its origin and spread. <u>Human Relations</u>, <u>1</u>, 464-485.

Jaeger, M. E., Anthony, S., & Rosnow, R. L. (1980). Who hears
what from whom and with what effect: A study of rumor.
<u>Personality and Social Psychology Bulletin</u>, <u>6</u>, 473-478.

Knapp, R. H. (1944). A psychology of rumor. <u>Public Opinion
Quarterly</u>, <u>8</u>, 22-37.

Koenig, F. (1985). <u>Rumor in the marketplace: The social
psychology of commercial hearsay</u>. Dover, MA: Auburn House.

Nkpa, N. K. U. (1975). Rumormongering in war time. <u>Public
Opinion Quarterly</u>, <u>96</u>, 27-35.

Prasad, J. (1935). The psychology of rumor: A study relating to
the great Indian earthquake of 1934. <u>British Journal of
Psychology</u>, <u>26</u>, 1-15.

Rosenthal, R., & Rosnow, R. L. (1985). <u>Contrast analysis:
Focused comparisons in the analysis of variance</u>. New York:
Cambridge University Press.

14

Rosnow, R. L. (1980). Psychology of rumor reconsidered.
Psychological Bulletin, 87, 578-591.

Schachter, S., & Burdick, H. (1955). A field experiment on rumor
transmission. Journal of Abnormal and Social Psychology, 50,
363-371.

Shibutani, T. (1966). Improvised news: A sociological study of
rumor. Indianapolis: Bobbs-Merrill.

Wiggins, P. H. (1985, February 14). Safeway rise and rumors. The
New York Times.

15

Appendix: Statistical Computations

## Negative Rumors

|      | low | mod. | high |
|------|-----|------|------|
| yes  | 11  | 11   | 31   |
| no   | 24  | 10   | 5    |
| $\Sigma$ | 35 | 21 | 36 |

|        | low   | mod.  | high  |
|--------|-------|-------|-------|
| $P$    | .31   | .52   | .86   |
| $S_P^2$ | .0061 | .0119 | .0033 |
| $\lambda$ | $-1$ | 0 | $+1$ |

$$Z = \frac{.31(-1)+.52(0)+.86(+1)}{\sqrt{.0061(1)+.0119(0)+.0033(1)}}$$

$$= \boxed{5.6701}$$

$$r = \frac{5.6701}{\sqrt{92}} = \boxed{.5911}$$

## Positive Rumors

|      | low | mod. | high |
|------|-----|------|------|
| yes  | 2   | 3    | 5    |
| no   | 6   | 4    | 2    |
| $\Sigma$ | 8 | 7 | 7 |

|        | low   | mod.  | high  |
|--------|-------|-------|-------|
| $P$    | .25   | .43   | .71   |
| $S_P^2$ | .0234 | .0350 | .0294 |
| $\lambda$ | $-1$ | 0 | $+1$ |

$$Z = \frac{.25(-1)+.43(0)+.71(+1)}{\sqrt{.0234(1)+.0350(0)+.0294(1)}}$$

$$= \boxed{2.0017}$$

$$r = \frac{2.0017}{\sqrt{22}} = \boxed{.4268}$$

# INDEX

abbreviations, 64, 80
*Abridged Index Medicus,* 23
abstracts in research reports, 42–43
active voice, 60
agreement of subject and verb,
    61–62
alphabetizing
    authors' names, 76
    reference list, 79
*American Doctoral Dissertations,* 30
American Psychological Association
    (APA), 18, 25, 29, 54–55, 76
ampersand (&) in citations and
    references, 75–76, 79
*Annual Review of Psychology,* 18
APA manual, 76
appendix in research reports, use of,
    42, 49
argumentative term papers, 3–4
Arnold, W., 19
art, 77–79
*Art Index,* 23
asterisk (*) to indicate probability
    level, 78
audience, 10
author cards, 15
automated card catalog, 14–16

*Beginning Behavioral Research:*
    *A Conceptual Primer,* 47
biographical resources, 30–31
*Biological Abstracts,* 23
Blanck, Peter David, 45
block quotations, 66–67
Bok, Sissela, 52, 56
Briggs, S. R., 45
browsing in library, 16–17
Buss, A. H., 45

Cacioppo, John T., 45–46
call numbers, 15
capitalization of references, 79
captions, figure, 77–78
card catalog
    automated, 14–16
    sample card from, 15
    use of, 14–19
charts. *See* figures
Cheek, J. M., 45
citations in text, 74–76
code letters and symbols
    in Dewey Decimal classification
        system, 16–17
    in ERIC, 24–25
    in Library of Congress classification
        system, 16–17
    in *Psychological Abstracts,* 21–23
    in PsycLIT, 25–28
    in *Social Science Citation Index,* 20–21
collective nouns, 61
colon, use of, 65
comma, use of, 64–65, 79
computers
    literature search and. *See* PsycINFO
        and PsycLIT
    modem access to PsycINFO, 18
    online catalog, 14–16
    word processing and, 50, 54, 68–69,
        71–72
Cooper, Harris, 47
copies of manuscript, backup, 68–69,
    72
correlational research reports, 5
Corsini, Raymond J., 19
*Current Biography,* 30
*Current Index to Journals in Education*
    *(CIJE),* 23, 25

117

TO THE OWNER OF THIS BOOK:

We hope that you have found *Writing Papers in Psychology,* 3rd edition useful. So that this book can be improved in a future edition, would you take the time to complete this sheet and return it? Thank you.

School and address: _____

Department: _____

Instructor's name: _____

1. What I like most about this book is: _____

_____

_____

2. What I like least about this book is: _____

_____

_____

3. My general reaction to this book is: _____

_____

4. The name of the course in which I used this book is: _____

_____

5. Were all of the chapters of the book assigned for you to read?     Yes     No

   If not, which ones weren't? _____

6. Do you plan to keep this book after you finish the course?     Yes     No

   Why or why not? _____

7. In the space below, or on a separate sheet of paper, please write specific suggestions for improving this book and anything else you'd care to share about your experience in using the book.

Optional:

Your name: _____ Date: _____

May Brooks/Cole quote you, either in promotion for *Writing Papers in Psychology*, 3rd edition, or in future publishing ventures?

Yes: _____ No: _____

Sincerely,

*Ralph and Mimi Rosnow*

FOLD HERE

------------------------------------------------------------------------

## BUSINESS REPLY MAIL

FIRST CLASS        PERMIT NO. 358        PACIFIC GROVE, CA

POSTAGE WILL BE PAID BY ADDRESSEE

ATT: *Ralph and Mimi Rosnow*

## Brooks/Cole Publishing Company
## 511 Forest Lodge Road
## Pacific Grove, California 93950-9968

NO POSTAGE
NECESSARY
IF MAILED
IN THE
UNITED STATES

FOLD HERE